Nāhiʻenaʻena
Sacred
Daughter
of Hawaiʻi

Nāhiʻenaʻena Sacred Daughter of Hawaiʻi

Marjorie Sinclair

The University Press of Hawaii Honolulu

Library of Congress Cataloging in Publication Data

Sinclair, Marjorie Jane Putnam.
  Nāhiʻenaʻena, sacred daughter of Hawaiʻi.

  Bibliography: p.
  Includes index.
  1. Nāhiʻenaʻena, Princess of the Hawaiian Islands,
1815?–1836.   2. Hawaii—Princes and princeses—
Biography.   I. Title.
DU627.17.N34S56   996.9'02'9024 [B]   76-27896
ISBN 0-8248-0367-1

But the record
           the palimpsest —
a little light
           in great darkness —

                    Ezra Pound

Burning burning burning burning
O Lord Thou pluckest me out
O Lord Thou pluckest

burning

                    T. S. Eliot

❧ Contents ❧

❧ Acknowledgments ❧

It is not easy to write the life of a princess who lived so briefly in an era when there were few written records. I had first to find and then piece together her sparse and moving story. Many of the records are to be found at the Hawaiian Mission Childrens' Society Library. There Elizabeth Larsen and Lela Goodell guided me to invaluable materials with skill and a continuing interest in the work. From Agnes Conrad, Hawaii State Archivist, I found much help with many of the obscurities I encountered. I am indebted to Janet Bell, Curator Emeritus, and David Kittelson and Yasuto Kaihara of the Hawaiian Collection who placed at my disposal the documents and materials of the Sinclair Library of the University of Hawaii. Two of my colleagues at the University, Professors Charles Bouslog and Leon Edel, read earlier versions of the manuscript and gave me invaluable criticism; I would like to thank them and also Mary Kawena Pukui, Professor Samuel Elbert, Professor Alfons Korn, and Dr. Alfred Hartwell who in various ways contributed to the detail of this work. I want to express my gratitude to Elizabeth Bushnell for her perceptive editorial assistance.

Two small segments of this biography, in other forms, have appeared in the *Hawaiian Journal of History*.

For permission to use the illustrations in this book, I am grateful to several sources. The photographs of the portrait of Kamāmalu and of the painting of the palace of Kamehameha III are from the Bernice P. Bishop Museum collection. The Hawaiian Mission Children's Society kindly provided reproductions of the photographs of Charles Stewart and Mrs. Richards and the portrait of Mrs. Stewart. The portrait of William Richards is in the collection of the Hawaiian Historical Society. The two old woodcuts showing the funeral of Keōpūolani are taken from Richards' *Memoir of Keopuolani*. All other illustrations are reproduced here by courtesy of the Honolulu Academy of Arts.

❧ Prologue ❧

Princess Nāhiʻenaʻena, though she lived in the early nineteenth century, is in many ways a prototype for those peoples of today who passionately want to preserve their ethnic identity: their dignity and their genius. Her life is prophetic of the anguish and the struggle of such people; but she herself went down in defeat, a victim of the collision of two cultures. Time is important in considerations of ethnic conflict: the past has played its role in creating the culture which trembles on the brink, if not of extinction, at least of exclusion; the present is the battleground; the future provides a hope for a life which accommodates the essence of the past to the continual metamorphosis that goes on in the flux of human affairs. Nāhiʻenaʻena was a witness to and an actor in the drama of that crucial moment when Hawaiʻi first confronted the men of Europe and America and learned to desire many of the skills these foreigners had. Her story shows that we must view biography and history both from within and from without, that they must be set in the culture in which the life is lived and the history unraveled.

It is difficult to find access to the culture of a people with an oral tradition. The voyagers, historians, ethnologists, sociologists who set down in writing their descriptions and chronicles often distort and often necessarily truncate. A society with an oral tradition has evolved its own language, its tradition, its imaginative response to racial and geographical experiences. A major problem in writing about the Princess Nāhiʻenaʻena has been that her history was largely recorded by those not of her race and culture. The data, consequently, present a limited and often biased view. There is probably little to retrieve now from Hawaiian chants and chronicles which would open for our understanding the essence of her life in some wholeness. We should therefore read the fragments that remain and fashion her biography as best we can to show her as a Hawaiian chiefess standing on the edge of her islands' first encounter with the good and the bad of Western civilization. She can become the symbol of an invaded culture which wishes to preserve in the world of today something of its identity and its uniqueness. Her biography is, in a sense, the biography of a symbol.

Her name means raging fires: *nāhi*, the fires; *ʻenaʻena*, raging, glowing, red. How write the history of a flame? In the chronicles of the world Nāhiʻenaʻena's life is less than a footnote. Hawaiian histories give her a sentence, a paragraph, a chance allusion. The fragments of her life are scattered in fading missionary letters, in brief passages written by early Hawaiian historians. They are transfigured into image and myth in a few surviving chants celebrating her. She is a mystery;

and yet she was a living girl, a royal person in a real Polynesian drama, a tragic figure.

When the fragments are put together, the story emerges;
often it sinks into forgotten days: one hears only the beat and
wash of the Pacific surf. Nāhiʻenaʻena's life has the frailty of
the old Polynesian culture: there remain crumbling stone walls
of ruined *heiau,* fishhooks, feather cloaks, bits of canoes,
songs that reveal and conceal passion and history. Yet a girl
takes shape, caught in a clash of cultures: we see the human
anguish of a princess of Hawaiʻi born into a proud, sophisticated, primitive culture who, at the age of five years, faced
also the power of Western culture. One childhood had to be
transformed into another. Nāhiʻenaʻena was like the delicate
crater bird which soars in its special island of air bounded by
volcanic walls and is suddenly caught in a downdraft, pulled
down into the fiery lava.

Who was Nāhiʻenaʻena? She was a child of Kamehameha I,
his only sacred daughter. Her mother was Keōpūolani, the
king's sacred wife. Her two brothers succeeded their father to
the throne. What was the source of her divinity? The ancestral
chants tell of her descent from the gods. The genealogies record generations of brother-sister marriages to link the royal
bloodlines. Her pride in this descent is reflected in the only
portrait of Nāhiʻenaʻena that survives, painted when the princess was nine or ten by Robert Dampier, an English artist. She
is dressed in a cape of red and yellow feathers edged in black.
In her small strong hand, she firmly holds a *kāhili,* a feather
standard, symbol of her rank. On her dark hair rests a coronet
of red feathers. The black eyes look directly at us. In them we
can see the girl—though she seems closer to fourteen than to
ten—and the woman she was about to become. The forehead
is smooth and the brows arched. The straight nose flares

slightly; the mouth is full and curved in classic Polynesian style. She carries her head proudly. In the landscape sketched behind, Dampier depicted the beauty of her island. A rich, spiked foliage, perhaps pandanus, frames her head. In the distance lies the village of Lahaina on Maui, with its lagoons, its grass houses, stone walls, and tall feathering coconut trees. Beyond stretches an azure sea; on it lies anchored a Western ship, ambiguous symbol in the life of the princess.

THE SACRED DAUGHTER, NĀHI'ENA'ENA, AGED 10
Robert Dampier

KAUIKEAOULI, AGED 11, LATER KAMEHAMEHA III
Robert Dampier

KAMEHAMEHA I
Louis Choris

KA'AHUMANU
Louis Choris

KAMĀMALU, FAVORITE WIFE OF LIHOLIHO
Artist unknown

LIHOLIHO, KAMEHAMEHA II
Artist unknown

HARRIET TIFFANY STEWART
Portrait 1822, New York

CHARLES S. STEWART
Photograph about 1863

WAILING FOR KEŌPŪOLANI
Left to right: Kuakini with cane, Hoapili, the Prince and Princess on the
shoulders of their *kahu*, Kamāmalu

FUNERAL CORTEGE FOR KEŌPŪOLANI
The foreigners are in front of the casket, the chiefs behind. The Prince and
Princess are immediately behind, followed by Liholiho and Hoapili

WILLIAM RICHARDS
Portrait about 1843

CLARISSA LYMAN RICHARDS
Daguerreotype about 1849

"VIEW OF PART OF LAHAINA IN MAUI"
Robert Dampier

"PORT OF HONOLULU in 1816"
Louis Choris

PALACE OF KAMEHAMEHA III, 1826
Watercolor by an unknown artist

Part I

1

"My Precious Object"

Most of what we know of the Princess Nāhiʻenaʻena was set down in the journals and letters of missionaries and merchants. The missionaries, notably Charles Stewart and William Richards, taught her her letters and introduced her to Puritan Christianity. The merchants gossiped about her. These were Western men, alien to her culture. What did Hawaiians say? The historian Kamakau chronicles small incidents of her life, but his accounts are often Western in tone. How, then, can we enter into the presence of the Hawaiian chiefess whom her people regarded as "the idol of the nation"? How can we know her as her people did? We can't, in actuality. But there are three surviving chants that give us clues. They celebrate her and reveal the reverence and the tenderness with which she was looked upon. For many reasons these poems are not easily read; they are filled with the *kaona*, hidden meanings, characteristic of Hawaiian poetry, with allu-

3

sions to which we no longer have the clue, with the ambiguity and obscurity of Hawaiian word and syntax.

The shortest chant is a *mele inoa*, a name-song, which Nathaniel Emerson records. A *mele inoa* honors a chief; it exalts his rank, sings of the qualities of his skill, records portions of his genealogy. This chant for the princess plays on the meaning of the name Nāhiʻenaʻena: *nāhi*, the fires, and *ʻenaʻena*, blazing. It begins by proclaiming her a chief among women. Then immediately the poet sets up a series of paradoxes as he puns on the "fire" in her name. "She soothes the cold wind with her fire. / A peace that is mirrored in calm." After this evocation of a rain-bearing wind which is calmed by flame (conventionally a cold wind is also a rainy one) the poet speaks of a life-giving spring in Kaʻū. Kaʻū is a place of vast lava fields where once the fires raged; now all is blackness and dust. But water that brings life bubbles through black sand. At the spring, which is so close to the sea that high tides cover the pool, the drinking dog barks at the incoming wave, the plants grow lushly—shrubs with scarlet flowers, green grasses and rushes. Near the spring is a blowhole through which the sea fountains. The blowhole speaks: "Who of right has the tabu?" The answer is Nāhiʻenaʻena. The poet concludes by mingling the image of the blaze of her name, *ʻena*, with red flowers rising in the water. "The flowers glow in the pool, / The bathing pool of Holei." Fire and wind and water are interfused in the poem. These elemental forces create a mysterious aura of power around the person of the princess.[1]

The two longer chants for Nāhiʻenaʻena were recorded by Abraham Fornander in his *Hawaiian Antiquities and Folklore*. "A Farewell to Harriet Nahienaena" suggests a drama of separation; in it there are constant shifts of mood, tone, voice—many people lament the princess' departure, but the focus of the feeling is intently upon the writer of the poem. It was composed by one who loved her, who was lamenting her return to Lahaina from Oʻahu. Without transition, he switches voices so that parts seem to come from the lips of Nāhiʻena-ʻena herself, as if she replies to the lament of the lover. There are many lines of direct statement of love: "Farewell to you, O Harriet / Great is the love for my friend / A love that knows no end." Many images suggest the intimacy of the relationship and hover about the places where the two were together. "Alas my close companion of the night;/ My sitting companion of the day;/ My companion in the cold." (Often in Hawaiian poetry coldness and rain imply an erotic relationship.) Nāhiʻena-ʻena's voice seems to answer: "Alas! my companion of the night;/ My *kapa* that kept me warm;/ My skin that was not cold when slept with in the night." The poem continues through 202 lines in which many places are named, many people and their affections are revealed; in which the writing of letters is mentioned. In spite of the obscurity of allusion, the mystery of the voices, the puzzle of the *kaona,* the poem reveals a warm love and the anguish of separation. The shadowy drama, staged after the departure of the princess, suggests the exchange of letters—one commenced at midnight and not concluded until the morning—friends clustering together to speak of Nāhiʻenaʻena and their love for her, the remembrance of places where the companions lingered and made love. The modern Western reader can grasp at least the picture of an intimate group of friends who express affection openly and the suggestion of a love affair which remains secret.[2]

The other chant in Fornander's collection is entitled simply "Nahienaena." The 145 lines are difficult, complex; the images gather luxuriantly. The tone is not intimate, but, in the manner of many chants for royalty, it celebrates and exalts the chief, linking him to the gods and creation. The poem seems to be arranged in sections, many of which are controlled by lines clustered around a single image or incident. The first section tells of the making of *kapa*. In this process, bark is softened with water, beaten into a kind of cloth, and finally decorated with vegetable dye. Different kinds of bark are described, the water bowl is named. The chief, the lines say, beats with a circular motion. In the process of beating, Nāhiʻenaʻena, who is symbolically both *kapa* and water bowl, creates a change in her elder brother, Liholiho. This change seems to lead to union: "The chiefs joined together the earth will be eternal." The chiefs, mingling their sacred blood, establish the stability of their kingdom: "While the chiefs join the earth abides firm."

After singing of the union of the chiefs, the poet chants of the sounds of nature's forces, especially the sounds of the sea, of thunder, the rumble of earthquakes, the noise of fine rain and heavy rain. Then the conch blows and the locusts sing shrilly. With typical quick shifts, the chant proclaims Kauike-aouli, the younger brother, to be the governor of the land, the one who was entrusted with the care of the island.

After the introduction of the younger brother, the poem returns to Nāhiʻenaʻena and the *kapa*. She stitches together the pieces of *kapa*, bites the thread, stitches and bites, stitches and bites. The sound of the *kapa* beater is like that of an adze, the beating makes a noise—a chief's *kapa* noise. And again Kauikeaouli enters the poem, this time as Nāhiʻenaʻena's companion. But it is she who enjoys the land. She is surrounded with images of nature; she lives upon the mountains and by the sea. Fishnets are cast and withdrawn, water bubbles up. Then someone seems to be climbing, breathing is dif-

6

ficult, the person begins to pant. And suddenly the poem speaks of sin. "The sin, the sin, let the sin be atoned for." The transgression, however, appears to be not of the Christians' sort but the breaking of a *kapu.*

Another sudden shift and the poem sings of the glory of the two young chiefs of royal birth. Nāhiʻenaʻena, walking with the heavy dignity of an ancient princess swathed in many layers of *kapa,* "issues forth as chief of the rising sun." The chant, having placed Nāhiʻenaʻena in the heavens, now recites fragments of mythic genealogy—how the chiefess and her brother Kauikeaouli are descended from the gods and the progenitors of the human race, Papa and Wākea. The poem takes on the quality and tone and content of a creation chant; it suggests the origin of earth and man.

Whatever the unfathomed meanings of this chant, some of the feeling and the symbolic equivalents are clear. Nāhiʻenaʻena is joined with her brothers in a physical and psychical union, one which brings good to Hawaiʻi because it brings stability and eternity to the islands themselves. She is the Resident of the land; she is a god who comes from the sun; she personifies the great human skill of the making of *kapa.* The poem's celebration of the princess encompasses her participation in ordinary human events, her chiefly prerogatives, and her descent from the gods.[3]

These three poems are all that remain to us—except for a few fragmentary accounts in Hawaiian historical writings—of Hawaiians speaking about their princess. The poems are traditional and reveal expected attitudes. It is impossible at this point in time to interpret them with any great clarity or detail because of the problems of secret meanings and of language. Yet they reveal, even in English translation, glimpses of the love which Nāhiʻenaʻena aroused in her people, their feelings about her *mana,* the divine power that still clung to her in spite of the abrogation of the *kapu* and the downfall of the ancient gods; they reveal the historical and sacred meaning embodied in the girl. She was the highest ranking woman in the kingdom, and in the very fact that she was a woman lay significance; there would be no doubt about children born from her body. They would carry the sacred blood.

The name-chant in its imagery reveals the paradox of her power, how her flame soothes the rain-bearing wind, how she brings water to the once fiery lava of Kaʻū. The farewell chant, personal in tone, suggests an intense love and strong grief at parting. She becomes in this poem a girl, not a chiefess aloof from her people. The final chant celebrates her and her two brothers as sacred chiefs. At times they seem almost to fuse, the three young chiefs, as a single power; they shared the sacred blood, and they were children of the great Kamehameha and the divine Keōpūolani, descended from the gods and from Hāloa, the first man. When the chiefs are joined together, as the chants say, the earth becomes eternal.

The earth was not eternal for Nāhiʻenaʻena and her brothers. Ships from the West had reached their islands. The ship that altered Nāhiʻenaʻena's destiny, and that of the Hawaiian kingdom, was the brig *Thaddeus* bearing the first company of American missionaries in 1820; the second company in 1823 brought the two missionaries Charles Stewart and William Richards, who would change the life of the princess. Of the two, Charles Stewart kept the most detailed record.

8

2

The
"Well-Behaved Child"

While Charles Stewart and William Richards were anti-
cipating their first landfall of the Hawaiian Islands, King
Liholiho, Kamehameha II, commenced a ten-day celebration
to observe the fourth anniversary of the death of Kamehameha I, his vigorous and shrewd father who had unified the
islands politically.[1] The celebration marked also the fourth anniversary of the young king's accession to the throne. Hawaiian feasts were noted for their length, their abundance, their
continuing pageantry. The king ordered a banquet table set in
a large pavilion erected for the occasion. The feast opened
with divine services—members of the first company of missionaries saw to that. More than one hundred guests sat at the
long table laid in "semi-civilized" style with a strange mixture
of shining gourds and Western china, wooden bowls and
glassware. The guests were also a mixture; Hawaiian royalty
and high chiefs sat down with the harbingers of a new way of

9

life — missionaries, merchants, shipmasters. The royal court had ordered Western-style dress, severely formal black; there had been gun salutes as for European royalty. The king's guard, dressed in Western uniforms and armed with muskets, stood at attention; but a group of warriors clothed in the brilliant red and yellow feather capes and cloaks of old Polynesia walked up and down. In the garden around the pavilion thousands of commoners gazed at this mixed magnificence of their chiefs.

The eight-year-old Princess Nāhiʻenaʻena was brought into the midst of the royal feasting. It was a moment of drama: she rode in a four-wheeled carriage "fantastically decorated" and pulled by servants. She was attended by chiefs of rank bearing tall *kāhili*, feather standards. When her equipage neared the banquet table, the king himself rose and helped to pull it. When it stopped, Liholiho lifted the child onto his back. He carried her to the table and seated her next to her brother Prince Kauikeaouli, the heir apparent. Facing his guests he announced, "This is my sister, the daughter of Kamehameha."

Charles Stewart and William Richards reached Hawaiʻi after a 158-day voyage from New Haven, Connecticut, aboard the ship *Thames*. In his journal Stewart writes of the long eagerness with which he awaited the landfall. The *Thames* in April 1823 entered the northeast trades and sped over the sea, two hundred miles a day. In the clouds at the horizon, the missionary fancied he saw the image of distant islands rising from the sea. On the morning of April 24, however, the cloud mass had greater stability; it seemed to be clustered about a headland. And by afternoon "the broad base of Hawaii, covered with Egyptian darkness, came peering through the gloom. The reality was too certain to admit a moment's question; and was accompanied by sensations never known before." In his heart Stewart felt pain mingling with the new sensations—the anguish of separation and the mystery of what lay ahead. Behind him was the old life in New Haven, the months aboard ship; he had developed a great affection for his fellow missionaries and for the sailors. But "the first tumult of feeling was quickly succeeded by something that insensibly led to solemnity and silence."

At evening the clouds dissolved and Stewart saw cultivated lands along the shore, forests in the higher regions, the shimmer of long waterfalls. "As the scene increased in interest and beauty, the language of our hearts was, 'Hail and welcome!' " After tea the missionaries gathered at the rail facing land to sing an old hymn.

> O'er the gloomy hills of darkness,
> Look, my soul, be still and gaze.

They were joined by the officers and crew. The sun set; the moon rose full in the east; "the haziness of the land suddenly gave way, without leaving a trace of gloom, which an hour before had overshadowed the whole Island, except a light drapery of clouds on the highest points of the mountains." The island lay spread before them. In the white light of the moon, Stewart thought of the moment as a divine sign, a revelation of hope for the work to come.

Charles Stewart appears as a serious, imposing looking man in the portraits that survive. The image of a younger man comes to us between the lines of his journals. He is romantic, intelligent, curious. He studied clouds and watched seashapes; he described Hawaiian pageantry, and he loved the

11

people. The young man had at first studied law in 1818; in 1821 he shifted to medicine, attending what is now Columbia University. Then apparently he had a religious call which sent him to the Princeton Theological Seminary, training place of many Calvinistic clergymen of the time. In 1821 he was ordained. A few months later, as missionaries in those days usually did, he married to have a helpmate in his life's work. She was Harriet Bradford Tiffany, a woman apparently of some social position, who was unprepared for the rigors of mission life. (The name Harriet would later be assumed by both Keōpūolani and Princess Nāhiʻenaʻena.) The young Mrs. Stewart dreaded leaving her family, dreaded having to live on a distant island among "savages." It is said that Stewart, in order to spare her the torture of tearing herself from her loved ones, took her driving in a buggy one day without telling her it was the time of sailing. He reached the ship and took her aboard. It was, in a sense, a spiritual as well as physical "kidnaping." Perhaps to mitigate the fears of his wife, or to ease her life in the strange new world ahead, he brought along a Negro woman who had once been a servant in the household of the president of Princeton College and had there fitted herself to be a Sunday School teacher. She would help in the Stewart household, but she would also teach. She came with them, not as servant, but as "humble Christian friend." This bringing of a dark-skinned woman from America as part of a missionary household was unusual; its psychological effect on the Hawaiian communities in which Stewart served can only be imagined. In any event, black Betsey Stockton was a proficient teacher of farmers and children in Lahaina. Stewart's devoted concern for his wife's welfare and his consideration for Betsey Stockton were carried over into his regard for the Hawaiians among whom he lived and worked.[2]

12

On April 25 the *Thames* neared the island of Hawai'i.
Charles Stewart at dawn gazed upon the "icy cliffs of Mauna
Kea" which "blazed like fire from the strong reflection of
the sun-beam's striking them." Engrossed in the beauty and
strangeness, he watched from the ship's rail; he felt the re-
moteness and mystery of these islands which he had seen the
night before clothed in gloom and which now gleamed in icy
fire. At nine o'clock the ship's deck rang with the cry, "A
canoe, a canoe!" And for the first time Stewart saw Hawaiian
people: "Their naked figures, wild expression of countenance,
their black hair streaming in the wind as they hurried the
canoe over the water with all the eager action and muscular
power of savages, their rapid and unintelligible exclamations,
and whole exhibition of uncivilized nature, gave them the appearance of being half-man and half-beast." When the canoes
drew alongside, the Hawaiians came on board to trade fish,
watermelons, bananas, sugarcane and sweet potatoes. By the
time they were ready to leave, Stewart's impressions had
changed; he spoke of their artlessness and simplicity, their
sprightliness and intelligence.

By midnight on Saturday the twenty-eighth, in the light of
the moon, the *Thames* reached the southeast end of O'ahu.
Once again Stewart's romantic sensibility was stirred. "Nothing can surpass the wild beauty of the promontories forming
the headlands of this part of the Island; and, I was detained on
deck, by the hour, gazing at them with delight." At sunrise the
ship was off Diamond Head, whose slopes Stewart described as
"fluted and furrowed from top to bottom by the washings of
water courses." As the *Thames* rounded Diamond Head,
Waikīkī stretched before it. The blue waters of the bay
sparkled in the morning light, and spume drift blew back from
the breakers; along the shore luxuriant groves of coconut

13

palms cast the shade of their restless fronds on sand and grass. Beyond the coconut grove, a broad, level plain spread out. "At the farther end of the plain, three or four miles distant, lay the town of Honolulu: to which, a fort with its floating banner, the American Consulate, the Mission-House and a cluster of masts in the harbour, gave something of an aspect of civilization."

When the *Thames* was opposite the village, Stewart peered at it through a glass. He mused on the stillness, "not the stillness of the Sabbath, though it was the day of God—but the stillness of a torrid clime." And he watched the natives lounging indolently among their thickly clustered grass houses— "so many sunburnt ricks of hay." He had indeed come to a "strange land."

The ship anchored off port, and the captain took a small party ashore—the three missionaries, Stewart, Richards, and Artemas Bishop, and two Hawaiian passengers as interpreters. They rowed along the coral reef, through the channel, and into the harbor. They made their way among a large number of whalers, native brigs and schooners to a long stone quay on which was a cluster of grass houses. They hoped to tie up there. Suddenly, however, people rushed from the houses crying, "*Kapu, kapu!*" The boat had stopped at the residence of the king, a forbidden place. The Hawaiian interpreters called out that a new party of missionaries had arrived. The natives reentered one of the grass houses, and presently appeared a "fine looking young female, in a European dress of pink satin, with a wreath of yellow feathers on her head." To the strangers she expressed regret that the quay was forbidden. She "politely requested us to row to a spot on the beach nearer the town, to which she pointed, and where she would meet us." Stewart soon learned that his welcome was indeed a royal one:

the young woman was Kamāmalu, the favorite wife of King Liholiho, Kamehameha II.

The queen awaited them with the American consul at the designated place. They landed and the consul made the formal introductions. In his journal, Stewart describes Kamāmalu's "fine black eyes," her dark hair, open and intelligent face, her tall, well-formed, masculine figure. It was his first view of the monumental stature (she was more than six feet tall), the dignity and grace of the chiefesses of Polynesia. He had, however, some reservations about her appearance: "Her features were too broad and flat for beauty."

Members of the first company of missionaries, who had arrived three years earlier, hurried to the landing place to greet their coworkers; the Reverend William Ellis, an English missionary, accompanied them. After the courtesies with the queen had been exchanged, the men of God, surrounded by a throng of singing, dancing Hawaiians, walked to the mission houses. In the quiet of the mission compound, the talk (we may imagine) was first of news from home, longed-for accounts of loved ones. But there was little time for conversation. It was the Sabbath day, and at eleven, divine services were scheduled in the chapel. Stewart could "never forget the excitement, with which I entered its lowly roof, trod the matted ground, its only floor, and looked at its unbarked posts and rafters, and coarse thatch of grass: primitive, as everything appeared, I felt it was a house of God."

After chapel, the new missionaries received a summons from a group of high chiefs living at Waikīkī, brought by the Reverend Hiram Bingham, of the first company of missionaries, and one of Liholiho's five queens. Stewart, Richards, and Bishop straightway set out on foot across the dusty plain to Waikīkī. The queen-messenger rode in a small wagon pulled by servants. Following her was the usual tableau of chiefdom: attendants carrying her symbols of rank, the fans, spittoons, umbrellas, and *kāhili*. The missionaries, however, walked in their stiff dark New England suits; it must have been a steamy three or four miles across the barren expanse to the grove of coconuts. At their right lay the sea, blue and glittering in the afternoon light, and at some distance to their left the green sunny cliffs of the Koʻolau mountains plunged into blue-shadowed valleys. Ahead of them lay the weathered slopes of Diamond Head.

The chiefs, encamped in leafy bowers in their favorite holiday spot, had assembled in one great lanai to greet the new missionaries. Among them were three of sacred rank, three who would play eventful roles in the lives of Charles Stewart and William Richards. They were Keōpūolani, the queen mother, and her young son and daughter, Kauikeaouli and Nāhiʻenaʻena. The Hawaiians lounged on piles of soft mats, some seated like Turks and some lying down, their heads on pillows of damask, velvet, or morocco. Each chief had attendants, one to fan, one to hold in readiness a polished wooden bowl filled with leaves—the spittoon—and one to flick away flies with a small feather *kāhili*. Each was dressed in European style, though the servants were in native garments. And each had a spelling book and slate at his side. Stewart writes: "They greeted us with much kindness of expression and manner; and seemed interested in the improvements they are making, and in the religious services of the day." After the introductions were over, the chiefs wrote their names on the slates to help the newcomers pronounce them. In turn they asked the missionaries to inscribe their names. "They repeatedly shook hands with us, reiterating their joy at our arrival, saying, they

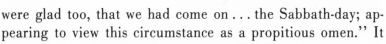

were glad too, that we had come on . . . the Sabbath-day; appearing to view this circumstance as a propitious omen." It was an omen of equivocal prospect for Nāhi'ena'ena.

King Liholiho was not to be seen, either in Honolulu or at Waikīkī. He was drunk. He still celebrated his festival of accession inaugurated a few days before.

At dawn on the second day after this visit ashore, twenty whaleboats towed the *Thames* into the harbor, and she was anchored opposite the compound of the king. Earlier, Liholiho had sent a message that he expected some of the new missionaries to call on him. Stewart and others promptly obeyed the royal command. They found the king in the dimness of a grass house, lying on a couch of silk velvet. He was dressed in only a chintz loincloth wrapped lightly about his waist. He was still intoxicated. His servants fanned him; one of his wives — probably the favorite, Kamāmalu — was offering him a cup of tea; he moaned, he tossed restlessly from his nausea. But he managed to indicate his pleasure at the arrival of the newcomers, and he asked the whole second company to call on him and the royal court later in the day.

At midmorning the missionaries and their families obeyed the royal command. They walked to the "palace," a new grass structure used for formal occasions; it had a door at each end, and down each side, rows of shuttered windows. When the missionaries entered, they saw a large room — there were no partitions — which was filled with a strange assortment of Polynesian and Western articles. The floor was spread with the finest of Hawaiian mats, soft to walk upon. On these mats, designed for bare feet and comfortable lounging, stood a rich array of Western furniture: mahogany tables, sofas covered in red Chinese silk, upholstered chairs. Mirrors hung from the grass

17

walls. Between them were "tolerable" engravings of European naval battles and two full-length portraits of Liholiho. Glittering above this ingenuous elegance were four cut-glass chandeliers suspended from the ridgepoles.

Most of the important chiefs, including those from Waikīkī, were assembled, making a "highly respectable appearance." Queen Kamāmalu of the brilliant eyes was engaged in official business. She sat on a sofa in front of a large table on which lay an open writing desk. At each end of the table worked a Hawaiian secretary. Commoners escorted by the king's bodyguard in groups of thirty or forty filed into the presence of the queen and "deposited their dollars" before her. The queen, Stewart realized, was collecting taxes! When she saw the missionaries, she rose quickly from the sofa and greeted them. "Her manners are dignified and graceful; and her whole appearance that of a well-bred woman, having an unaffected expression of conscious and acknowledged rank." Kamāmalu, however, was businesslike. The amenities observed, she returned to her work.

The missionaries joined the assemblage of chiefs, where chairs had been placed for them. Not until they were seated did Kaʻahumanu enter. The favorite wife of Kamehameha I, a woman of volatile but forceful temperament, she wielded significant political power in the nation. Her official title was *kuhina nui,* words difficult to translate into English. In actuality she shared the rule of the kingdom with Liholiho—as she had proclaimed during the formalities of his inauguration to the throne. The chiefess walked with "much of real majesty in her step and manner." She wore a *pāʻū* made of many yards of yellow satin wrapped and folded from her waist to below her knees. Over one shoulder a *kīhei,* or cape, was draped; it fell behind her into a train. On her head she wore a tiara of wreaths of yellow, red, and blue-green feathers. Her face, Stewart wrote, revealed "sternness and hauteur."

After Kaʻahumanu, the royal children, Kauikeaouli and Nāhiʻenaʻena, entered. The prince was dressed in a coat and pantaloons of black silk velvet. Stewart, who chronicles the ceremony, devoted his attention to the princess. He had first seen her at Waikīkī. On this second view, he describes her, and the tone of his writing reveals the special attraction she had for him, an attraction which was felt by many others, Hawaiian and foreign. Nāhiʻenaʻena was carried, in the traditional way for youthful ranking chiefesses, on the shoulder of a stalwart man. He had crossed his arms over his chest to make a firm resting place for her feet. To steady herself she encircled his forehead with one arm. Her costume was European—a somber one for a girl of eight; it was fashioned of black satin with gold lace; on her head she wore a black satin hat decorated with feathers. Her appearance suggests European royal children in eighteenth-century portraits, small princes and princesses transformed by clothing into miniature adults. Stewart comments, "She is a pretty and well-behaved child, not as an Indian, but according to our own ideas of the characteristics of childhood."

The king, though present, was not yet sober. The missionaries proffered their official papers to the high chiefs and distributed simple gifts; within the hour the formalities of their arrival had been concluded. Not until several days later did Charles Stewart see a sober Liholiho. Dressed in a fashionable navy blue suit, a beaver hat, and Wellington boots, he called on the captain aboard the *Thames*. He affably waived the harbor fees for the ship because she had transported new teachers to Hawaiʻi. His manners were "polite and easy, and his whole deportment that of a gentleman."

Charles Stewart and the second company of missionaries were present to see the brilliant spectacle which concluded Liholiho's celebration in honor of his father and himself. It took the form of a procession, a kind of wayward parade full of color, music, the shouts of excited people. Each chief created his own pageant and his own bit of drama, while the commoners danced and chanted along the edges of the various routes. Stewart watched and recorded; he was deeply stirred and recognized with some regret that such an "exhibition of ancient customs . . . probably will soon be lost forever in the light of civilization and Christianity, now rapidly dawning on the nation."

He writes first of Queen Kamāmalu. She was not only Liholiho's favorite wife, but his half-sister—and the half-sister of Nāhiʻenaʻena. Though a daughter of Kamehameha, her rank was not divine, for her mother had not been Keōpūolani, the sacred wife. The meaning of her full name, Kamehamalu, memorialized her great father: "in the shadow of Kamehameha." Kamāmalu rode in a whaleboat which had been draped and festooned with yards of elegant *kapa* and foreign materials. Her vehicle was fastened to a platform and was borne by a solid phalanx of men. They were dressed in scarlet and yellow feather cloaks or capes, and on their heads were feather helmets similar in shape to that of Achilles as depicted on Greek vases. With the queen in her equipage stood the prime minister and the national orator dressed in *malo* (loincloths) and feather helmets. Each carried a thirty-foot *kāhili* of scarlet feathers. Kamāmalu wore Hawaiian dress—a *pāʻū* of red silk draped from the waist to the knees and on her head a feather lei. She was shaded from the sun by a large Chinese umbrella of crimson damask. Her rank on this occasion was carefully distinguished by the size of her equipage, the presence of the prime minister and the national orator, and shining displays of feather robes, helmets, and standards.

The other queens of Liholiho rode in double canoes carried as litters. They too were dressed in the traditional *pāʻū* and wore leis of feathers. One of them, Pauahi, staged a small drama, a startling and blazing moment. She stopped her entourage and, dismounting from the canoe, set it afire. Then she unwound the many yards of her skirt and heaped them on the flames, keeping a "handkerchief," as Stewart puts it, to cover herself. Her attendants honored their mistress by adding their skirts to the fire. Pauahi's action was not merely a whim; it was staged to remind all present of her escape from a blazing grass house when she was an infant, an escape also perpetuated by her name: *pau*, end; *ahi*, fire.

The royal children, Kauikeaouli and Nāhiʻenaʻena, were borne on a litter of strange fabrication. It consisted of four carved Chinese bedsteads lashed together, richly covered with the finest quality of *kapa* and ornamented with festoons of yellow moreen. At each side of their vehicle marched several high chiefs who carried tall *kāhili* of state; behind the children, like servants, walked two distinguished men: Hoapili, their stepfather and second husband to Keōpūolani, and Kaikioewa, the guardian of the prince. Hoapili carried calabashes filled with raw fish and poi, while Kaikioewa carried a platter of roast dog—royal children grew hungry during long hours of procession. Kauikeaouli wore the traditional *malo*, and Nāhiʻenaʻena, a *pāʻū* of scarlet silk.

On this final day of his celebration, the king had no pageant. He was drunk again. Dressed in a *malo*, he rode unsteadily on a horse, his suite of favorites following him. They careened in mad disorder up and down the various paths of the procession while the royal bodyguards tried, at running

21

march, to stay close to their master. The commoners, delighted with the confusion, shouted and chased along.

The procession followed no formal route; each chief with his elegantly draped litter, his feather standards, noble attendants, and servants traveled his own winding course through the town of Honolulu. Troops of singers and dancers festooned with leis of flowers and leaves roamed at random. Whenever they saw a favorite chief, they surrounded his entourage and forced a halt. Chanting and dancing, they celebrated the personal beauty and distinguished ancestry of the honored person. Throughout the day, the throb of drums, the pulse of bare feet, the shouts of the commoners, the recitative of chants, and a film of dust hung in the air of Honolulu.

Charles Stewart, who had first viewed Hawaiians as half-man, half-beast, was caught up in the strangeness, excitement, and beauty of much that he saw on that day. "I doubt whether there is a nation in Christendom, which, at the time letters and Christianity were introduced could have presented a *court dress* so magnificent as these. . . . There is something approaching the *sublime* in the lofty noddings of the *kahilis* of state." He had come all the way from New Haven to find himself abruptly plunged into a day-long pageant that seemed almost like a fairy-tale, or an account out of some old book written by voyagers long ago—a fairy-tale in which grim things were mingled. Beyond pageantry lay the call of duty. The romantic in Stewart had had a feast for eyes and senses: the solemn priest had other and more somber thoughts.

3

Keōpūolani,
Sacred Mother

We do not know exactly when Nāhiʻenaʻena was born; the historians say 1815.[1] We do not know the place, perhaps it was Keauhou on the island of Hawaiʻi where Keōpūolani had a residence and where Kauikeaouli had been born in March 1814 (some say in 1813).[2] The only surviving detail is that Keōpūolani insisted, contrary to custom, upon keeping "this last child" under her own guardianship. Though Nāhiʻena-ʻena was installed in a household of her own, as were all infant chiefs, she remained under her mother's watchfulness, as she approached the brink of a new era.[3]

We know a great deal more about the birth of her brother Kauikeaouli, and it may give us clues to some of the rituals observed at the time of Nāhiʻenaʻena's birth. While Keōpūolani was pregnant with her last son, many chiefs asked for the privilege of bringing up the child. This was traditional; but the sacred queen refused. Was it in her mind to keep this baby, as she later kept his sister Nāhiʻenaʻena? Or did she wait for a chief who might let her share in the baby's rearing? She recalled how Kamehameha, some fifteen years earlier, had placed Liholiho in the charge of Kaʻahumanu, his favorite wife, and how all her other babies—those eleven or twelve whose lives were not long—had been taken from her. Then Kuakini, one of her guardians and a distinguished chief, came to Keauhou. When he requested the child, she consented. But she asked him to remain at her side until after the birth so that no one else could take possession of the infant. Kamakau, the Hawaiian historian, writes: "On the night of the birth, the chiefs gathered about the mother. Early in the morning the child was born, but as it appeared to be stillborn, Kuakini did not want to take it. Then came Kaikioewa from some miles away . . . and brought with him his prophet who said, 'the child will not die, he will live.' " The baby was washed and laid in a consecrated place; the prophet fanned him, sprinkled him with water, and recited a prayer in which the boy was linked, as was appropriate to his sacred rank, to the gods:

> The heavens lighten with the god,
> The earth burns with the child,
> O son, pour down the rain that brings the rainbows,
> There in heaven is the Lord.
> Life flows through my spirit,
> Dedicated to your law.

When the prayer was over, the child moved; he began to cry— he was alive! The seer gave the baby the name Keaweaweʻula, the red trail. It signified "the roadway by which the god descends from the heavens." But Keōpūolani gave him two names of her father's, Kīwalaʻō and Kauikeaouli, and entrusted the boy to the care of Kaikioewa.[4]

Nāhiʻenaʻena too, as the child of the sacred Keōpūolani, provided a pathway to the gods. And the chiefs gathered around for the royal birth, ready to offer themselves as guardians. The strong-minded queen, however, kept this child for her own — probably over considerable protest at this departure from tradition, particularly the tradition for a divine child. One of the chants which have been referred to traces Nāhiʻenaʻena's genealogy back to the first man and woman, back to the gods. Throughout the poem, allusions are made to Kauikeaouli and Nāhiʻenaʻena as companions to whose keeping the land is entrusted. The sacred brother and sister were thus surrounded from infancy with implications not only of divine origin but of divine marriage as well.

To understand Nāhiʻenaʻena's short and passionate life, we must know something of her father, and more especially of her mother. Her father, the great Kamehameha, had been a courageous and successful warrior. He knew well how to manipulate the *kapu* to his advantage, though he himself carefully observed them; how to handle the chiefs, the commoners, the many Westerners. He recognized the expertise and the power in Western gunnery, carpentry, and trade; he recognized the desirability of a relationship between nations, and he sought an alliance with Great Britain. His sacred daughter was born only four years before he died. Though Nāhiʻenaʻena knew her father and was continually reminded of his greatness, Kamehameha could have remained in her consciousness only an impression, an affection she owed, a distinction of which she could be proud: a dim childhood memory.

Her mother, however, endowing her with divine rank, gave her some of the important guiding forces of her life. Keōpūolani possessed a strong nature and an ability to act forcefully. She was born in 1778,[5] a momentous year for Hawaiʻi — Captain Cook saw his first Hawaiian landfall in that year. She died

in 1823, a Christian convert. Her life journey, though span-
ning a short forty-five years, was a passage from the intricacies
of Stone Age culture and the worship of idols, across the
threshold into Christianity and into the complexity of Western
culture.

The parents of Keōpūolani had been half-brother and
-sister, the children of a chiefess of sacred rank. They mingled
the royal bloods of the islands of Maui and Hawaiʻi and endowed their daughter with a divine *kapu,* surrounding her
with the awesomeness of a god. She went out only at evening
or night so that no one could step on her shadow; the unlucky
one who did so would be put to death.[6] One of her ancestors,
according to legend, had been transformed into a goddess, a
water deity. The image of this goddess with all its powers
descended to Keōpūolani, and when she came under Kamehameha's protection, he honored this idol and displayed it
on his battlefields and during state occasions. Later it was said
that the power of his sacred wife's god enabled him to unify
the islands.[7]

Keōpūolani grew up in the dual world of a sacred chief. She
lived with the human realities of days spent in grass houses,
with constant ceremonial, near the battlefields of war waged
by the chiefs—the brutal stab of spear, blow of axe, and
necessity of flight—and with the poor health which most records claim she suffered throughout life. She lived also in the
world of the divine, and as a god was kept at a remove from
most mortals. Her childhood was thus primarily an entangle-
ment of the sacred and the warring. She was four when her
father was killed in conflict with Kamehameha, thirteen when
she came into the possession of the warrior king, seventeen
when he married her. Though she was booty of war, so to say,
she was not a slave princess. Kamehameha observed her *kapu;*

she had a household of her own; she was honored with appropriate ritual. After the marriage, the great king removed his *malo* and prostrated himself in her presence. As offspring of the sacred wife, her children would carry on the dynasty he had established.[8]

In her role as Kamehameha's queen, born with the "fire" *kapu,* comfortable in the awareness of her special kind of power, Keōpūolani displayed courage and resolution. She began to take actions against the very ritual which was symbolic of her divinity, but which was also imprisoning. Both Kamakau and William Richards report that she sheltered persons who had broken the *kapu* and that men came to her for sanctuary. She allowed no one—if she knew of it—to be put to death because he had violated her divine *kapu.*[9]

History knows Keōpūolani best for her breaking of the "eating *kapu.*" This bold action, taken when Nāhi'ena'ena was a child, was a major thrust in the overthrow of the old gods and the elaborate structure of precept and obligation. To understand the significance of Keōpūolani's symbolic gestures, one must recognize that the eating *kapu* was at the core of a system of law, of prohibitions and permissions, which provided structure and control in Hawaiian society. The word *kapu* means forbidden. A man, an act, or an object could be *kapu,* sacred—belonging to the gods; there was danger in being near or in touching it. Persons or objects might be *kapu* because they were in themselves corrupting. Thus, as in other cultures, women were considered threatening at the time of menstruation and childbirth. Periodic or temporary *kapu* were often invoked: some regulated supplies of fish or plants; some were imposed by priests; some were proclaimed at the whim of a chief, perhaps to celebrate a significant date in his own or his family's history. Two rules of the eating *kapu* in particular vexed the great chiefesses. One forbade certain foods to women, such as pork, bananas, coconut. The other prevented men and women from eating together.

On the day of Kamehameha's death, Keōpūolani publicly broke this important *kapu*: she ate coconut, and she sat down with the chiefs to dine. She announced to them, "He who guarded the god is dead, and it is right that we should eat together freely."[10]

She acted about a month later with greater drama, staging her revolt during a feast in celebration of Liholiho's accession to the throne. Keōpūolani sent a messenger to the chiefs' banqueting place to summon her younger son, the heir apparent, to come to the women's eating hall. The new king himself brought his young brother to his mother. Liholiho stood at the threshold and watched as the boy Kauikeaouli entered and sat down to eat with the women. The king, however, remained outside the pavilion. He was not ready to take a move which could undermine the source and the power of his royal position. In the weeks that followed, Keōpūolani, together with Ka'ahumanu, the prime minister, the high priest, and others, continued to urge Liholiho to abrogate the eating *kapu*. He hesitated for several months. Then he acted with abruptness and a show of drama which seemed, as did so many of his actions, highly impulsive. A great feast of the forbidden foods was prepared. The men and women were to dine in the same place, but the tables of the chiefesses were separated from those of the chiefs. While the preparations were going on, Liholiho caroused in a sailing canoe with his favorites. At the hour of the banquet, he came ashore. He entered the feasting place and walked about. Then abruptly he sat down with the chiefesses and ate. A great shout arose, *'ai noa!* free eating. Before the banquet was over, the king had sent out messengers to declare the *kapu* abrogated. He commanded that the images and temples be destroyed. The old order, the order from which Liholiho had his power, had been abolished.[11]

It was a great change, though in some ways a subtle one, and it could not take effect in reality by proclamation alone. For the mass of Hawaiians it represented too sudden a break with the past. And many were puzzled by the actions of their sacred queen—she who had the highest rank of any person in the kingdom. This was later expressed by Kamakau, their historian, who wrote that it was "strange that Keopuolani should have desired free eating against her own interests and those of her children. She and they were looked upon by the people as gods with powers like fire, heat, light."[12]

Gods with powers like fire and light: We may wonder why Nāhi'ena'ena's mother wanted to give up the privilege of deity, even though it surrounded her with restrictions. There had been no missionary to influence her, for the first company had not yet arrived. But Keōpūolani had simply looked about her; and she saw the reality. She saw, as did many other Hawaiians, that the foreigners broke the *kapu* and no god smote them down. Some of the chiefs had already eaten forbidden foods and had survived. What was the power of such gods? Keōpūolani appears to have recognized the fallibility of the old order.

The queen also recognized another reality—the value of reading and writing. These were skills the Westerners brought, along with their new knowledge and their kind of wisdom. Keōpūolani accordingly urged her three children to study their letters—especially after the missionaries had established a school in Kailua, Kona, in 1820. Though the queen did not immediately accept the religious teachings of the men of God, this attitude did not cloud her recognition of what she might learn from them. As the months went on, she observed the men themselves. She saw much that appealed to her: that they established schools as well as churches, the manner in which they cared for the sick, their devotion to their God, and their hatred of rum. Though she enjoyed rum, she knew its evils. She had watched her son Liholiho in his drunken antics and sufferings; there had been times when he seemed near death from his excesses.

In the last year of her life, Keōpūolani turned to the Christian faith. She began to study reading and writing; she learned to pray, and she took instruction in religious doctrine. She became convinced that the real power was to be found in the Christian God and that His Son had died for her.

The mother of Nāhiʻenaʻena lived only long enough to take a first impressive step into Western culture. But she wanted to make sure that her daughter would become a civilized woman. The queen attempted to chart, as best she might, Nāhiʻenaʻena's future. Her dying charge directed the little girl away from the Polynesian rituals of her infancy and early childhood into the complexity of Western, Christian civilization.

4

"Dark Heart"

During the period of Kamehameha's dying and Liholiho's accession, the image of Princess Nāhiʻenaʻena remains in shadow. She is not mentioned in the known surviving accounts, but we can assume her presence — a sacred child in the court circle. The missionaries were the first to paint her picture — only a few brush strokes to begin with, later a more detailed portrait. The missionary writings of 1820–1822 do little more than mention her name. When members of the royal family are listed, she is called the king's small sister. After the arrival of the second company of missionaries in 1823, Charles Stewart and William Richards chronicled much of what we know about her, for they were entrusted with her education. They came to love her; and they were deeply distressed to learn how quickly she could yield to impulse and how troubling was the confusion of her spirit.

We first see Nāhiʻenaʻena shortly after Liholiho moved his

court from Kailua, Kona, to Honolulu. The king, with the advice of the council of chiefs, had decided to establish the seat
of government on Oʻahu, primarily because of its fine harbor
and thriving trade with merchants and whalers. The royal family arrived from Kailua and Lahaina—where they had made a
short stop—early in 1821; Honolulu immediately celebrated
with a round of feasts and dances.[1] On February 22, 1821,
Maria Loomis, wife of the missionary printer, writes of going
to a "splendid dance" honoring in particular the "granddaughter of the late king," a girl of seven or eight. She does
not mention the name Nāhiʻenaʻena, and she speaks of a
granddaughter. Kamehameha, however, referred to his children by Keōpūolani as his grandchildren, just as he had referred to Keōpūolani as his daughter, although she was his niece.

The dancing took place, as Mrs. Loomis describes it, in an
open area, tree-shaded and spread with fresh rushes over
which mats were laid for the chiefs. When the missionaries arrived, the chiefs were already seated in their places, and a hundred soldiers carrying muskets and bayonets stood at attention. Around the edge of the area, in trees, on the ground, two
thousand commoners jostled and pushed and waited for the
spectacle. At a signal, the soldiers marched off, half to the left
and half to the right: the moment had come for the entrance of
the princess. She rode on the shoulder of a husky man, followed by a retinue of eight or ten attendants. She seated herself in the place of honor in front of the company of chiefs.
Mrs. Loomis does not describe the child. Her brief record suggests that Nāhiʻenaʻena conducted herself with an awareness
of royal privilege, that chiefs and commoners alike acknowledged the drama of her presence. A "splendid dance" was
performed by three young girls. Their dance was accompanied
by ten men who beat formal rhythms on sticks and chanted

32

mele. Mrs. Loomis was told that the songs celebrated the glory of the princess.

The missionaries left before the performance was concluded. On their way out, they saw—and registered their shock—a wooden image lying on the ground. It was that of Laka, goddess of the dance. Liholiho had overthrown the gods, but he could not drive old loyalties from the hearts of his people. They clung to Laka, deity of the woods and of the dance, a benign and gracious spirit, and Hawaiian dancers continued to dedicate themselves to her worship.[2]

Although there is no further mention of Nāhi'ena'ena during the years 1821 and 1822, we can attempt to reconstruct some parts of her life. In Honolulu she was established in a household of her own; a retinue of chiefs and friends attended her, as was customary for one of her rank. Queen Keōpūolani insisted that she study her letters regularly, and we know that by 1823 Nāhi'ena'ena could read and write.[3] The queen probably took her daughter to chapel services and prayer meetings, especially during the period when the venerable chiefess developed an interest in Christianity. Life for the princess, however, must have continued in many of the ancient patterns. She listened to chants honoring her ancestry; she watched dances for her entertainment. And there were long idle hours devoted to surfing, talking, napping, lounging with the small chiefesses of her ''court.''

Nāhi'ena'ena's girlhood was not harassed by the warfare which set boundaries to her mother's. Other forces marked her boundaries, at times sharply, definitely, at other times vaguely. She was living in a society uncertain of its values and laws; the *kapu* had been abolished; she was learning European and Christian ways. She was a princess—but a princess neither of the old Polynesian world nor of the nineteenth-century Western world. She and Kauikeaouli continued to be kept apart from all but those of suitable rank, continued to be celebrated together in ceremony. These moments of parade or royal audience showed very simply the ambiguities: on some occasions she was dressed in a *pāʻū,* a feather cape on her shoulders and feather coronet on her head; on others, she wore a satin gown and gold-fringed bonnet. Beneath this outward show, what lay in the heart of the girl? We can only study the casual notes, the brief descriptions and short comments. Three forces appear to emerge. One was love for her brother Kauikeaouli; this love was in the ancient mode—the devotion of two young high chiefs, brother and sister, growing up in expectation of linked destinies. Another was Keōpūolani's movement toward Western religion and attitudes and her consequent desire that Nāhiʻenaʻena might grow up to be "like the wives of the missionaries."[4] The third was the study of writing and religion under the missionaries themselves. These men were both stern and gentle; they insisted on a religion-centered life and attempted to cultivate in her a Christian humility. Nāhiʻenaʻena floundered in enthusiasm, doubt, and rebellion as she faced the Western influences.

In 1823 the girl—partly because of her mother's actions— moves more clearly into our view. Keōpūolani, in failing health, determined upon a removal from Honolulu to the quieter coconut groves of Waikīkī. With her she took Hoapili her husband, Nāhiʻenaʻena, and all the many lesser chiefs and attendants of her household. In the cool air, near the gentle-sounding surf, she would find the quiet to continue her study of Christian doctrine, to pray, to talk with the Western men of God. Each Sunday a missionary walked the hot plain from Honolulu to her encampment to hold divine service. But these services soon were not enough, and the dowager queen asked for a religious teacher to be in residence in her household. A Tahitian who had come to Hawai'i with the English missionary William Ellis was appointed. His name was Taua.[5]

The entrance of Taua into the queen's retinue created some foreseeable opposition. In Keōpūolani's large household were chiefs who clung to the old order; they were disturbed by the influence of the missionaries and Taua on their sacred chiefess, and they attempted sporadically to separate her from the new religion. William Richards chronicles a morning when Keōpūolani, feeling weaker than usual, decided to remain on her mat for further rest; she asked her attendants and the chiefs to leave so that she might have an hour of prayer alone. The chiefs were astonished. Alone? An *ali'i kapu*? They laughed, Richards says, perhaps in unbelief, that she should ask for their withdrawal. The queen sternly reprimanded them and "told them they still kept their dark hearts." She then explicitly ordered them to leave, and they obeyed.[6]

Keōpūolani wanted also to release Nāhi'ena'ena from the "dark heart" of the past. Hiram Bingham writes that the queen asked that her daughter be trained in the ways of missionary wives and civilized women. Bingham recognized that it would be difficult to protect the girl from the traditional influences, that it would be impossible to separate her entirely from her own people, especially in view of the conditions in the Hawaiian kingdom at that time.[7] We cannot know how much Nāhi'ena'ena felt or understood the conflict closing in on her life. As an intelligent girl of eight she must have observed a great deal: the strife surrounding Taua; the extravagant, disorderly, drunken life of her king-brother Liholiho — a life openly criticized by Keōpūolani and the missionaries; the Christian piety of her mother, surrounded still by the ancient symbols of her sacred rank; the austere simplicity of life among the devout men and women her mother so much admired. Nāhiʻenaʻena found herself running a gamut of glory and obedience: one day she was a royal child, clothed in splendid garments and carried on parade; another day she obediently copied a spelling lesson on her slate, or humbly bowed her head in prayer. She was in the very center of contradictions.

In May 1823 Queen Keōpūolani moved again. This time she went to Lahaina, on Maui, the island of her birth. Again Nāhiʻenaʻena and Hoapili and a large group of chiefs accompanied her. Before leaving Honolulu, the queen asked the American missionaries to send someone in addition to Taua to pray with her and to preach—she wanted a mission established on Maui. Charles Stewart and William Richards were named for these tasks. Nāhiʻenaʻena, by her mother's action, was thus withdrawn from the turbulence and pageantry of the royal court and placed in the relative seclusion of a provincial town, with men of God for company.

Stewart's journal records his arrival on Maui. From the deck of the handsome *Cleopatra's Barge,* the ship in which the king had sent his mother, the missionary looked with delighted eyes at the landscape. Lahaina was not a Honolulu, not a dusty village on a barren plain. It was a verdant haven, set dramatically between green, precipitous mountains and a cobalt sea. "The entire district, stretching nearly three miles along the sea-side, is covered with luxuriant groves, not only of the cocoanut . . . but also of the breadfruit and the *kou* . . . while the banana plant, *kapa,* and sugar-cane are abundant and extend almost to the beach, on which a fine surf constantly rolls." The thatched houses peeped "from beneath the

36

broad leaves of the plaintain"; the coconut palms nodded "like plumes in the breeze" against the "noble exhibition of mountain scenery in the distance."[8]

On the day after Stewart's arrival, a Sunday, Keōpūolani sent a messenger to the missionaries in the early morning announcing that she, the princess, and the other chiefs were ready for worship. Stewart and Richards hurried to the *kou* grove at the beach where the queen mother's temporary lanai had been erected; more than three hundred people had gathered—reverence for the queen mother was far-reaching. Before this congregation, the missionaries celebrated the first Sabbath in Lahaina. Under a blue sky within the sound of surf, Taua read the scriptures in Tahitian and the Americans conducted divine service. Keōpūolani asked the two missionaries to come every day at sunrise and sunset to say prayers for herself and the princess.[9]

On the following day, in the households of the chiefs, schools were established by the queen. By the end of the first week on Maui, Stewart was able to write that Hawaiians might be seen morning, noon, and night "in groups from ten to thirty persons, spelling and reading and writing . . . whether in their houses, or in the grove, whether strolling on the beach, or I might almost add sporting in the surf."[10]

Early one morning about a fortnight after the arrival on Maui, the queen again summoned Stewart and Richards to the beach. They found her with the Princess Nāhiʻenaʻena; and standing at a distance was a group of workers with a pile of lumber. Keōpūolani and the princess greeted the missionaries cordially and conducted them to one of the sites which had been discussed for the mission building. The queen had made her decision. But she first asked approval from the men of God—and they gave it. Immediately the workers began to dig the holes for the house posts of two grass buildings. Stewart writes: "Our kind patroness remained on the ground till we ourselves left it for breakfast; and constantly addressed us and spoke of us to the people by the affectionate appellation of 'sons.' "[11]

The Lahaina days of the royal chiefesses were not devoted entirely to prayers and schools. Stewart describes an afternoon in late June when he was returning from a visit aboard the ship *Boston* of Nantucket, anchored in Lahaina Roads. He noticed that many Hawaiians had gathered near Keōpūolani's residence and that others were hurrying toward it. He followed them and found the queen, the princess, and other chiefs seated on their mats in the shade of the *kou* trees. Several young girls in costumes of yellow *kapa*, richly folded and draped from the waist to the knee, were dancing. On their heads and around their shoulders the girls wore leis of fresh forest leaves and flowers, on their wrists bracelets of ivory, and around their ankles ornaments of dogs' teeth, which rattled like castanets. The musicians, all male as usual, beat the intricate rhythms of the dance on huge gourd drums and chanted *mele* in a kind of recitative. Occasionally the dancers themselves joined in the singing. "The motions of the dance were slow and graceful, and, in this instance, free from indelicacy of action; and the song . . . was dignified and harmonious in its numbers." The words celebrated Keōpūolani and Nāhi'ena'ena and compared them to "everything sublime in nature"; the two were exalted, Stewart commented, as if they were gods.

So rapt with the dance were the spectators that the missionaries, always mindful of their duty, began to wonder how they could gain attention for evening prayer. Keōpūolani, however, did not forget. At the moment of sunset, she ordered the performance to stop, the people to be seated and to remain silent. Stewart and Richards then conducted evening prayer before a congregation of two thousand.[12]

William Ellis records a similar dance a week or two later. Ellis, a veteran in the Pacific, recognized the flowers and leaves that garlanded the six dancers — gardenias and *maile*, a sweet-scented vine. He too comments on their "modest propriety." However, at the time of evening prayer, he did not hesitate to preach about "their former idolatrous dances, and the vicious customs connected therewith."[13]

One afternoon late in June, a sail was seen in the channel between the two islands of Lānaʻi and Molokaʻi. As the ship came closer, five shots rang out — it was the private signal of the king. Though the commoners gathered on the beach, the chiefs and missionaries held the usual sunset prayer. After the service, Stewart and Richards escorted Nāhiʻenaʻena and Liholiho's youngest wife, Kekauonohi, to the shore. At about the time they reached the beach, Liholiho jumped from the ship's boat to the sand. He first greeted the missionaries. Then he embraced his wife and sister and, putting an arm around each, strode to the *kou* grove to greet his mother.

There the chiefs had assembled in the traditional formal circle to await the king. Liholiho paused at the edge of the circle opposite his mother. Stepping inside, he knelt to embrace a chiefess, the mother of Kekauonohi. The chiefess, deeply moved by the king's action, burst into tears; she rose immediately and led Liholiho to Keōpūolani. Stewart describes the meeting. "He knelt before her, gazing silently in her face for a moment, then pressed her to his bosom, and placing a hand on each cheek, kissed her twice in a most tender man-

39

ner. . . . I scarce ever witnessed an exhibition of natural affection where the feelings were apparently more lively and sincere. The king is a fine-looking man, and graceful in his manners; while gazing on him, the queen's heart seemed to float in her eyes, and every feature *told a mother's joy.*"

At sunrise next morning Stewart and Richards went as usual to the queen's house for the prayer service. Empty liquor cases were stacked on a mat in front of the queen's residence; bottles littered the ground. They could find no queen, no princess, no congregation. Here and there men and women slept in the heavy stupor of drunkenness. The frustrated missionaries returned home. Shortly before noon they came back. But the revelry had begun again—"We quickly turned from so melancholy a scene of licentiousness and intoxication." The king had brought his favorites and cases of liquor from Honolulu; friends from Lahaina had joined in the merry-making.

At sunset the missionaries tried once again to find their royal congregation. But Liholiho's party had commenced. "The wild and heathenish sounds of the song and dance" throbbed in the evening air. This time Taua approached and explained that Keōpūolani waited at the residence of Nāhiʻenaʻena. Stewart and Richards hurried to find the usual group of worshipers and "pupils." Keōpūolani was resting on a couch. She was in tears. She lifted her hand and pointed toward her home in the *kou* grove. Then in a voice shrill with feeling, she cried, "Shameful, oh shameful!" Unable to face the missionaries at this moment, she leaned back on her couch and hid her face against a roll of *kapa* to sob. Stewart and Richards waited for her to recover her composure; then Taua read the evening prayers. He called upon God to send His grace to Keōpūolani and begged Him to lead King Liholiho to reformation and redemption.

On the evening of his arrival in Lahaina, Liholiho had moved into his mother's house and had begun to enjoy his usual entertainment of drinking, music and dance. His mother had pleaded with him to stop, but the king had refused. Thus in the middle of the night she had left her residence and gone to Nāhiʻenaʻena's. Before leaving she warned her son that his behavior would bring him to "the everlasting fire."

Stewart records a conversation between Keōpūolani and her son which might well have taken place that night, the drums beating accompaniment. Liholiho accused his mother of studying too much; it was not good for her, he claimed. "You are old and it is well for you to study only a little." Keōpūolani admitted that she was indeed old. "Soon I shall die; therefore I must learn soon, or I shall die before I obtain the good thing I desire."

Liholiho showed his irritation, especially at the stern rules set down by the missionaries; the rules separated him from the old comfortable relationship with his mother. He pointed out that the missionaries did not allow them "to do anything we formerly did. Their teachings are false and evil, their prayers are not good. Let us return to our former custom; let us now, as we formerly did drink a little rum together."

Keōpūolani defended her teachers. She reminded her son that once he had said the missionaries were good and that he had instructed her to cast away the old religion and listen to them. Now it was he who disregarded their teachings. She defied the king: "I will never forsake my teachers. I will never take my dark heart again."[14]

The conflict between the queen and Liholiho had broader implications than a dispute between mother and son. It was a sign of the complexity and contradiction in the growing disorder spreading through the kingdom, as customs, attitudes, and ideas of Westerners met Polynesian patterns. Taua was a small example of Western influence. Not only was he a Christian convert, but as chaplain in the household of Keōpūolani he was turning the old queen from the traditions of the past. Nāhiʻenaʻena was already entangled; she showed moments of confusion.

First Fruit
of the Mission

In September 1823, Queen Keōpūolani's illness grew worse: a large abscess had grown between her shoulders, and she was subject to "spasms" that filled her family and attendants with alarm. At times, when she fainted, those at her bedside believed that her last moment had come. The chiefs, summoned from all the islands, crowded into her grass house; the king, the young prince and princess, and Hoapili were in constant attendance as they listened to her faint words and comforted her. In that grass house was the atmosphere of awe and grief, of solemnity, which attends the deathbed of any person of eminent birth and accomplishment.[1]

Outside, the commoners gathered in the *kou* grove. They sat, they listened, they wailed. The wailing for the dead was traditional. But with it there ran an undercurrent of nervousness and fear. The death of a sacred chief in Hawai'i was usually attended by violence. Many who came to mourn were prepared if necessary to flee. The missionaries, spectators for the first time of a royal death among the people to whom they ministered, watched with strong curiosity and emotion, and wrote of the event in their journals. We have a fairly vivid picture of Keōpūolani's last days and of the ceremonials that surrounded her death. Charles Stewart, full of affection for this first and major convert, called as frequently as decorum permitted. He described how he found on one occasion fifty chiefs crowding around the queen, lifting up their voices in that strange wail so difficult to describe, intense, anguished, mysterious. He wrote with astonishment and a sense of history — this must have been the way the people of Israel wailed in their tents long ago. Stewart tells of a young chief, known for his stern composure, who knelt by the queen and greeted her with tenderness; then the tenderness gave way to grief as he saw her wasted with illness. The chief lifted his head and wailed "in a manner that would have touched any heart."[2]

The king's surgeon, Mr. Law, formally told the people early in September that the queen mother would probably not survive this illness; this sent a cry among the waiting people that she was already dead. A messenger rushed to the mission house with the news. Charles Stewart, together with Mrs. Stewart and Mrs. Richards, hurried through the darkness to the queen's house. They were greeted with silence: the chiefs were sitting on their mats, most of them in tears. Keōpūolani was alive but very weak. "She reached her hand to the ladies" and spoke of her affection for them. She thanked them for coming through the night to visit her. She whispered, "I love God. Great is my love for God."[3]

Keōpūolani had prepared herself for death. Her two vital concerns were her commitment to the Christian God and the future of her children. When the prime minister, Kalanimoku, reached her bedside, William Richards recorded that she repudiated the old gods, saying to him, "Jehovah is a good God. I love him, and love Jesus Christ. I have no desire for the former gods of Hawaii. They are all false. But I love Jesus Christ." She commanded her subjects to show restraint in their mourning, to control the ancient frenzy of sorrow which had traditionally been marked by relaxing of the *kapu*. On such occasions, mourners sometimes mutilated their bodies, knocked out their teeth or pulled out their hair; sometimes they indulged in sexual orgies. The queen ordered that her body be buried with Christian decorum. The flesh was not to be stripped from the bones and the bones secreted in a cave, as was done with those of Kamehameha and of the high chiefs of her own long ancestry.[4]

Keōpūolani seemed deeply anxious about Nāhiʻenaʻena. A few days before her death, she summoned Hoapili to her bedside. She said: "See that you take good care of Nahienaena. See that she is instructed in reading and writing, that she may learn to love God and Jesus Christ." On the day before her death, she talked to Kalanimoku about her two younger children. "I wish much that my two young children Kauikeaouli and Nahienaena should know God, should serve him and be instructed in Christianity." She asked him to take care of the prince and princess and not allow them to associate with evil companions.

On one of the last days she spoke to her children and the assembled chiefs. "I am now about to die. I shall leave my children, my people, and these lands, and I wish now to give you my last charges." She asked the king her son to be a friend to his father's friends and to hers. He must protect the lands, the people, and the missionaries. She urged him to keep the Sabbath and serve God. And again she stated: "I love

45

Jesus Christ. I hope he has loved me, and that he will receive me." Keōpūolani had done all she could as queen and mother in her preparation for death.[5]

Most of all, during these hours of the death watch documented for us by the missionaries, the suffering queen asked that water "be sprinkled on me in the name of God before I die." This wish for baptism was ardent; but the missionaries, in their insistence upon the letter of the law, could not comply. It was not that they did not want to welcome her into the church. The embarrassment was that in Lahaina they had no ordained interpreter fluent enough to provide the queen with the simple dialog necessary for the holy ceremony. As Richards recorded, the circumstance was "peculiarly trying." Soon it would be too late; Keōpūolani, as she drifted toward death, moved her body only slightly and was only occasionally aware of those around her. The missionaries continued to watch and pray. The answer arrived in the person of William Ellis, the English missionary, who came to Lahaina to join the mourning people. A veteran worker in Polynesia, with long service in Tahiti, a natural interest in native lore, and a fluent mastery of Tahitian and Hawaiian, he appeared to be a messenger sent from God. He could grant the queen's last wish. The missionaries hurried their colleague to Keōpūolani's bedside. She was asleep. Twice they returned in the hope of finding her awake. But she slept. Liholiho, with his sharp sense of reality, could not understand such hesitation. Was it not simply a matter of sprinkling water and uttering some prayers? "What is the harm?" he asked. But Ellis and his companions waited for signs of consciousness. Baptism could not be administered to those who slept — the proper words could not be spoken. They returned to the mission house.[6]

The waiting was heavy and filled with thoughts of the uncertainty of what the royal death might bring. A messenger suddenly arrived, crying in terror that the queen was dead. The missionaries set out for her house. The gathered Hawaiians had begun to flee in every direction, over walls, through taro patches, clutching calabashes or pieces of *kapa* filled with their belongings. Fearing for the ladies who were alone at the mission, Stewart returned, while Ellis and Richards hurried to the queen's residence. Ellis, more experienced in Polynesian ways, bowed to the logic of the chiefs' urgent request and agreed to sprinkle water on the queen in the name of God. The entire mission family accordingly gathered in the royal house. Keōpūolani was breathing regularly. She gave little sign of recognition; she did not speak. The king issued commands for absolute silence. Around Keōpūolani's couch stood the family, the high-ranking chiefs, the missionaries, and merchants. Mr. Ellis made preparations for the holy ordinance. He delivered a short address in Hawaiian to define baptism; he explained why it was being administered to Keōpūolani. Then, after the prayers, he performed the act; the queen in her death coma was sprinkled with water and the name she had chosen for her baptism was pronounced — Harieta (Harriet), she had selected the Christian name of Mrs. Stewart.[7]

Queen Keōpūolani thus became the "first fruit of the Mission." The ceremony was performed at five on the afternoon of September 16, 1823. An hour later Keōpūolani died.

At nine the missionaries returned to the royal household to conduct evening prayer. As they walked along the beach, they found that all was quiet in the encampments of the chiefs. Near Keōpūolani's residence, however, a large group of people wailed. The family remained at the side of the corpse. The small prince and princess "appeared entirely inconsolable."

Hoapili had wrapped his arms about them, and when the missionaries entered, he included Stewart in the embrace. He spoke somberly. "Keopuolani, our friend, is gone to heaven, and we, alas! are left alone."[8]

Keōpūolani's funeral mingled the old and the new. There were the sounds of grief: minute guns were fired, bells tolled, the people wailed. Charles Stewart described the sounds of wailing—*auwe, auwe,* alas! alas!—the last syllable drawn out in a trembling and anguished voice, high or low, shrill or soft. The sound of the word was accompanied by a variety of gestures. Some wailers stood, their arms and faces toward the sky, their eyes closed. Others clasped their hands behind their heads. Still others stooped until their faces almost touched the ground; their hands were braced against their knees or were held to their sides as if they suffered from internal pain. Some seized their hair as if to pull it out. By the time Kuakini, governor of the island of Hawaiʻi and distinguished elder statesman, had arrived for the funeral, about five thousand people were gathered near Keōpūolani's house. The burst of wailing was so intense when he appeared that the minute guns could not be heard.[9]

An old print in the Richards memoir of Keōpūolani portrays the scene. In the background stand three grass houses, stark and barnlike. At the queen's house, the Hawaiian flag flies at half mast. In front of the houses, multitudes of people are shown wailing. The prominent figures of the foreground are Governor Kuakini dressed in foreign clothes and leaning on a cane, Hoapili and Kamāmalu in Hawaiian garb, and the young prince and princess. The children are seated on the shoulders of attendants and are dressed in foreign style. Little Kauikeaouli has his hands and head raised toward the sky and wails. His sister Nāhiʻenaʻena holds on to the forehead of her attendant; her head is thrust back, her mouth wide open uttering her sorrow. Even in the stiff, somewhat naïve drawing, the scene suggests desolation and grief.[10]

The funeral, a Christian one, was concluded with a royal procession. Four or five hundred people marched, including the American consul and other distinguished foreigners. The casket of the queen was covered by a black pall and was attended by the five queens of Liholiho and the daughter of Hoapili, each holding a black *kāhili*. Immediately behind the body of the queen walked Kauikeaouli and Nāhiʻenaʻena. This time they were not carried in the usual fashion. A print in Richards' memoir offers us the picture — a long black line of mourners and the royal children, small and almost lost behind the casket with its ceremonial display of tall black feather standards.

After the entombment in a house of mud and stone, the chiefs settled down in temporary residences where they lived for several weeks. This was their way of honoring the sacred queen, of remembering her last wishes and showing their love. During their stay, they built a stone wall around the mausoleum. In symbolic action, they took the stones from a nearby *heiau*, a temple for the old gods. The Princess Nāhiʻenaʻena did her share. Stewart describes her: the small girl carried a large stone while a stalwart man walked behind her bearing a *kāhili* of state.[11]

The princess carried another burden for her mother, one she could not yet understand. Keōpūolani had bequeathed to her daughter the difficult task of reconciliation; she had left the child to cope with the pain and confusion of clashing worlds. In the surviving accounts of the queen's last month of life, we see the princess huddling close to her mother's side and sobbing. She listened when her mother spoke; she re-

49

membered for the rest of her life the Christian and Western charges Keōpūolani laid upon her. She was not, however, a child alone among towering elders. Her brother Kauikeaouli was with her at the royal bedside and marched with her in the funeral procession. The prince and princess, as before, were set apart, isolated in their own world as sacred children.

Keōpūolani's death marked a critical moment in Hawaiian history. The last of the sacred chiefs born in the old order was gone; Liholiho was freed from his tender obligation to his mother. The inevitable changes would come rapidly.

In the Absence of the King

Liholiho decided almost immediately after his mother's death to fulfill a desire he had long felt, one probably aroused in him by Kamehameha when he was a boy. He announced to the chiefs that he would travel beyond the Pacific horizon to see the places and wonders he had studied in his geography lessons. He wished to visit England in particular. The chiefs accordingly met in council at Lahaina to discuss the wishes of their king.[1]

We know the king was a restless man; he was also an extremely inquisitive one. The restlessness was, perhaps, bred into him as sacred chief, heir apparent to the throne; he traveled from *heiau* to *heiau*, from battlefield to battlefield, from island to island. After he became king he continued to travel, even though he officially established his court in Honolulu. His restlessness increased with the increasing pressures of Western culture on the kingdom; then perhaps it became another means—along with rum—of escaping from perplexities and responsibilities.

His desire to go to England was not restlessness alone. It was a very real curiosity. He had long shown a mind capable of taking in and retaining details and facts about other lands. William Ellis, who was not only missionary but an amateur anthropologist, tells us that Liholiho talked "with no small accuracy" about lakes and mountains in North and South America, about the men and elephants of India, about England, its houses and manufactured products. "I have heard him entertaining a party of chiefs for hours together, with accounts of different parts of the earth." Once when Liholiho opened his writing desk, he commented to Ellis that he expected "more advantage" from the desk than from one of his ships anchored in the harbor. His particular wish to visit Britain stemmed from a tenuous tie between England and Hawaiʻi which had been negotiated by Kamehameha I. Liholiho hoped for a personal interview with the British king so that he might place "himself and his dominions under British protection." He wanted also to study the English system of administering justice—a serious problem in the Hawaiian kingdom—and to inform himself about Western practices in commerce.[2]

Many of the chiefs were reluctant to let their monarch go on this mysterious voyage into the unknown. But the will of the king prevailed. He accepted the offer of Captain Valentine Starbuck, American master of a British whaleship *L'Aigle*. Starbuck could take only a small number of people, as his ship was already loaded with 2,200 barrels of oil. Liholiho chose as his traveling companions his sister and favorite wife, Kamāmalu, the high chief Boki, governor of Oʻahu, and Boki's wife Liliha, his treasurer Kekuanaʻoʻa, his admiral Kapihe, and John Rives, interpreter. *L'Aigle* sailed from Lahaina to Hono-

lulu, where the final arrangements were made, not the least of
which was the outfitting of the monumental Hawaiian royalty
in clothes of silk and satin suitable for a European court.

During the council of chiefs at Lahaina, Liholiho settled the
matter of securing the Kamehameha dynasty. He proclaimed
his younger brother heir apparent. Kamakau writes that he announced, "Where are you, Chiefs! I am about to sail to a foreign land and I place my younger brother Kauikeaouli to be
your chief. I go, and if I return, I return; if not, then you are to
have my younger brother as your king." To the boy he said,
"Live in peace with the chiefs; those lands which belong to me
are yours, the lands given to the chiefs shall be theirs."
Though Liholiho had divested the chiefs of the power of the
kapu, he had not taken from them that steady and lasting
power, the land.[3]

No Hawaiian king had ever ventured into that far-off sea,
the Atlantic, or to that far-off country, England. Their ancestors had remained in Pacific waters crossing great expanses of
ocean, and for centuries the Hawaiians had lived their sea-girt
lives and made local journeys from one island to another.
Chiefs and commoners alike sensed the drama and the danger
of their king's purpose. On November 27, 1823, the day of embarkation, the people of Honolulu moved restlessly about on
the beach; many wailed as if for a death. Guns from the fort
fired in salute. *L'Aigle,* plying back and forth outside the harbor, waited for the boats to bring Liholiho and his suite.
Queen Kamāmalu stayed on shore longer than anyone else;
she sat on a mat with her beloved relatives and friends. Reluctantly she rose, at the last, embraced her mother and the
others with tenderness, and walked slowly through the crowds
to the quay. There she turned and asked for silence. She said,
"I am going to a distant land, and perhaps we shall not meet

53

again." Then she raised her arms and chanted a farewell to
her country.

> O heaven! O earth!
> O mountains and sea!
> O commoners and people!
> Farewell to you all.
> O soil, farewell!
> O land for which my father suffered,
> Farewell,
> O burden that my father strived for.
> We two are leaving your labors.
> I go in obedience to your command,
> I will not desert your voice.
> I go in accordance with the words you spoke to me.

She stepped into the ship's boat. The wailing grew louder, and
the cannon roared from the fort. The queen was rowed to the
whaler; and the crowds saw *L'Aigle* spread her sail and move
out to sea. "As its mast sank on the horizon the faces of those
on board disappeared as if going down into the grave." So
wrote Kamakau (Bingham also used the image of the grave in
his account), reflecting the feelings of the people.[4]

The mast of *L'Aigle* disappeared below the horizon; the
young prince and his sister, heirs to the throne of Kamehameha, remained behind, surrounded by their guardians and
courtiers. Had Hawaiʻi been a European country, in another
century, the children's lives might have been in jeopardy; one
remembers how wandering kings left behind them heirs who
became the center and victims of court intrigue. But Hawaiʻi
had no Tower in which little princes and princesses might be
locked up; and there seemed to be no struggle for power — at
least sacred royal power — among the regents. The king was

absent; his return was a matter of time. Ka'ahumanu had held the position of premier with great skill and strength after Kamehameha's death, and Liholiho's absence if anything consolidated her authority. In the court circle, Hoapili had his influential role as guardian of the royal children and trusted friend of the great Kamehameha; he had his own province as honored high chief. Kīna'u had her particular place as a secular daughter of Kamehameha; however she had less *mana* than her sacred half sister Nāhi'ena'ena. Any political struggle behind the scenes during Liholiho's absence was certainly not a struggle for the throne. The monarchy was solidly established and in recent years had been centralized. The struggle appeared in reality to be between the missionaries, powerfully ensconced as educators of royalty as a consequence of Keōpūolani's religious passion, and those chiefs who were not yet prepared to yield the age-old traditions and prerogatives of the Hawaiians. The children of Keōpūolani were caught between the influence wielded over them by their educators—the reverend personages from New England—and that of the Hawaiian leaders who from time to time sought to pull the royal heirs back into Hawai'i's past, and into their sacred blood-roles.

Nāhi'ena'ena continued to make Lahaina her home after Liholiho's departure. Hoapili, her stepfather, remained her guardian; Charles Stewart and William Richards were her teachers. Missionary accounts reveal that early in 1824 the Lahaina chiefs—the princess included—showed a renewed enthusiasm for knowledge; for the first time they expressed a desire to share the skills of reading and writing with "all their subjects." From the beginning, the chiefs had claimed exclusive rights over these skills. In February, Stewart and Richards, making one of their frequent calls on the chiefs, found them intent upon their studies. Nāhiʻenaʻena and some of Liholiho's queens were writing at their desks; seated around them on mats their attendants wrote or worked in spelling books. In the flush of this enthusiasm, many chiefs ordered that "neat and spacious schoolrooms" be built next to their houses where servants and farmers could gather three times a day to learn to read in Hawaiian. Stewart could discover no reason for the sudden eagerness, which increased the demand for Hawaiian books. Americans, particularly the missionaries, could not yet understand the whims of chiefs who allowed, as the historian Kamakau observes, their thoughts to flow wherever their desires were centered.[5]

The renewed interest in learning was accompanied by a revival of religious ardor, if this can be measured by the numbers attending worship. The missionaries preached to much larger congregations. David Malo, however, was skeptical. This Hawaiian historian-scholar commented, "Aye, a great many people, but they come not to hear the good word perhaps but only to see the dress of the chiefs." And the chiefs put on a bright show: in place of the shining feathers and delicate *kapa* of the past, they now wore fashionable European clothes. They had discovered in church meetings an outlet for their traditional love of color and procession. One may imagine the childhood beauty of Nāhiʻenaʻena on these occasions. Perhaps she worshiped in the very church her mother had ordered built and which had been inaugurated during the last month of Keōpūolani's life — a plain grass church near the sea. A missionary account says that before church services a chair upholstered in either crimson or green was customarily readied for her. She arrived dressed in a velvet or satin European gown, attended by a *kāhili* bearer and maids of honor. She sat

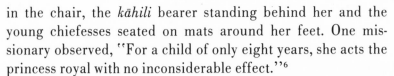

in the chair, the *kāhili* bearer standing behind her and the young chiefesses seated on mats around her feet. One missionary observed, "For a child of only eight years, she acts the princess royal with no inconsiderable effect."[6]

With the summer heat in Lahaina, the interest in *palapala*, letters, and *pule*, prayers, declined sharply. But not only surf and azure air diverted the chiefs' interests. They had become deeply troubled: the chiefs, even the young ones, were dying at a frightening rate. Liholiho's absence intensified their anxiety; they had watched him vanish, and to many he had seemed at that moment to be going down into death. William Richards, in a letter to Boston on June 1, 1824, pointed out that of thirty high chiefs, ten had died in two years. "Some say it is the *palapala*," he wrote. A boy in Lahaina had dreamed that the sickness among the chiefs was caused by Kauikeaouli's confining himself too much to study. The boy's dream proposed a remedy. The prince must make a tour of the island and stop at each village to order a public cockfight. If he did this, the sickness throughout the whole island would cease. Kauikeaouli, naturally, was delighted at the prospect, and some of his attendants and lesser chiefs agreed. His guardian, however, was of a different mind. "I am the guardian of Kauikeaouli. When he desires to go around the island for any good purpose, he may go. But he shall never go in obedience to the command of the devil."[7]

The native anxiety manifested itself in another way—in a desire to secure the royal line. In June the council of chiefs assembled in Lahaina to discuss the suitability of a marriage between Nāhi'ena'ena and Kauikeaouli. During a morning session, Kalanimoku, the prime minister, talked with Elisha Loomis about the propriety of brothers marrying sisters. Loomis explained that such a marriage was immoral. Kalanimoku countered with the statement that it had been the custom among the highest chiefs from ancient times. Loomis used every argument at his command: incest was forbidden by the word of God in all civilized communities; moreover, the children of brother-sister parents tended to be "weak and sickly." Just what Kalanimoku reported to the council of this conversation we do not know.

During the afternoon session, the chiefs again discussed the proposed marriage of the prince and princess. Alarmed, Loomis and Richards went to the meeting place. The chiefs explained that there were no young people of suitable age and rank in the kingdom for Kauikeaouli and Nāhiʻenaʻena to marry; it was of supreme importance to keep the royal blood pure. The missionaries repeated their most forceful argument; they pointed out that frequently there were no children to such a marriage, and the few that were born were usually weak and sickly. When asked if they had known the off-spring of such a union, the chiefs replied that Keōpūolani's parents had been brother and sister. The missionaries reminded them that she had been sickly and had died at an early age. We do not know the ultimate conclusion reached by the chiefs or whether or not the missionaries were told of it. Loomis, however, recorded the meetings in his journal. He observed also that Nāhiʻenaʻena seemed to have arrived at puberty early, and remarked that the people of Hawaiʻi matured more rapidly than those in temperate climes. He and others noted the emotional disturbances of the princess. She acted impulsively, wept easily, followed quick enthusiasms, swung from mood to mood. In his record of the talks with the chiefs, Loomis says explicitly that it was well known that Nāhiʻenaʻena and Kauikeaouli had been for some time living together "in a state of incest."[8]

This was probably true; it would be remarkable if it were not. Only about a year and a half apart in age, the royal children had grown up as if they were husband and wife from the first. "Though the prince is heir apparent, yet the princess is equally honored." Furthermore, it was traditional in Hawaiʻi that brothers and sisters of high rank should love one another. Ancient legends and chants told the stories of such love. Kamakau wrote that "women in those days were especially devoted to their brothers, and brothers to their sisters. It was common to see younger sisters sitting in their brothers' laps. Brothers chanted verses composed in honor of their sisters, and sisters of their brothers as a sign of devotion."[9]

These serious conferences concerning the future of the prince and princess which took place during the king's absence had as their counterpart a strange festival. The festival revealed the restlessness of the Hawaiians and their apparent desire to tear loose from the bonds of the missionary world that Keōpūolani had so warmly accepted and sealed at her death. A year had passed since the day when the queen, the "first fruit" of the church, had been interred; and the court gave out that the royal children wished to commemorate the occasion in a fitting manner. The original missionary accounts are on the whole meager and matter-of-fact. Motivations were not explored; however, an ambivalent mood prevailed among the Hawaiian leaders. The leaders were quoted as saying that the occasion was "only the play of children." If so, it was very sophisticated "play" indeed for a boy and girl not yet ten years of age. Some claimed that because the prince and princess had no superiors, absolute permissiveness was necessary. This, of course, was a deceptive rationalization; the royal pair had always been controlled by both their guardians and their missionary teachers. High political motives could be discerned behind the "play of children" in this court of powerful figures. It seems hardly likely that Ka'ahumanu, Hoapili, Kaikioewa, Kīna'u would leave such matters to children; and the scale of the celebration, its symbolic overtones, its very setting, showed significant links with the past and bespoke a great malaise. What it essentially expressed was hostility to the missionary world which had brought bleakness and rigidity to the formerly relaxed court. One may imagine that in the absence of the king, the missionaries had taken advantage of their prime position of power over the children, and that a struggle, perhaps subterranean, existed between the proponents of the old, as against the power of the new. The scale of the festival reflected the planning of wise old Hawaiian courtiers; the prince and princess were too young to think in such elaborate terms. In a word, the festival was an assertion of the sacredness and *mana* of Kauikeaouli and Nāhi'ena'ena, for at that moment they were the supreme symbols of Hawai'i's past.

With an inbred sense of drama the prince and princess (but in reality it could only have been their advisers) chose for the commemoration the very grove of *kou* trees which had framed the final setting for Keōpūolani. The celebration itself was one of rejoicing rather than of mourning, and it had far-reaching consequences. A large mahogany table was laid with fine china and glass for thirty people. At each end stood a sofa upholstered in crimson damask, royal seats for Kauikeaouli and Nāhi'ena'ena. Chairs for the guests were similarly upholstered. At one side had been erected a platform thirty feet long, covered in fine *kapa*. In the middle of the platform "a kind of throne was formed . . . as another seat of honor for the princess." On the other side of the table the stewards and servants waited with calabashes of food to serve the guests. The calabashes were elaborately draped in red, green, or yellow nets hung with tassels and green vines. Stalwart men holding *kāhili* were stationed at intervals around the feasting place. The commoners, held back by a fence and armed guards, gathered in large numbers at the edge of the grove; groups of singers and dancers put on random performances in the crowd.

The first person to enter the grove and take her place was Kīna'u, daughter of Kamehameha and a queen to Liholiho, a chiefess of considerable political power. Dressed in the ancient fashion, she was swathed in so many heavy layers of *kapa* that she needed attendants to support her and carry the trains of her *pā'ū*. Another queen, similarly dressed, followed her. The very fact that they chose *kapa* rather than European clothes or fabrics had its significance. Kauikeaouli entered with fanfare. The doors of the nearby fort abruptly opened, and a guard and drum corps marched out, the military vanguard for the heir apparent. The boy appeared, dressed in a purple suit trimmed in gold, a dagger hanging from his belt. In attendance upon him, a young chiefess sang and danced as he marched along the route of the procession. After the prince, Nāhi'ena'ena came, dressed in Hawaiian garments. She rode on a litter covered in a hundred thicknesses of *kapa* and borne by twelve chiefs. "She was shielded from the sun by lofty Chinese umbrellas of rich damask, and surrounded and followed by several of the larger kahilis as the insignia of her dignity." The children's procession did not directly approach the banquet table where the celebrants would take their seats; it moved several times between the fort and the grove. Each time she reappeared, the princess had made changes in her dress and was surrounded by a new group of attendants. Stewart records, "The air rung with the shouts of the multitude and with songs in her praise."

61

Whatever the implications surrounding the festival, it had disastrous consequences. The banquet ended in general drunkenness. And the drunkenness was a signal for a break-down of more of the missionary tabus. The people of Lahaina gleefully returned to some of their old sports, particularly gambling and boxing matches, which often led to violence and death. The disorder was not confined to Lahaina; it swept through the kingdom. By late September Kaʻahumanu was so alarmed that she moved to restore order. Criers were sent throughout the islands to announce that drunkenness, theft, and murder were forbidden; that all people must observe the Sabbath; that schools must be established and people learn the *palapala*.[10]

Whether Kaʻahumanu and the missionaries liked it or not, the patterns of the past demanded a moment of attention. Nāhiʻenaʻena herself was more deeply involved in the resur-gence of the old than in the celebration of her mother's death. In October, shortly after the *kuhina-nui*'s proclamation, the princess wished to dispose of some of her dresses. The pos-sessions of a chief had always been carefully guarded in the past and then disposed of beyond reclaim; it was believed that a sorcerer who laid hold of even so little as the trimming from a royal fingernail could pray that chief to death. To insure Nāhiʻenaʻena's safety, the dresses were packed in weighted boxes and secretly taken out to sea to be "buried." A rumor started, however, that one dress had been stolen. Nāhiʻena-ʻena's attendants became alarmed; they concluded that the princess was already subject to a sorcerer's spells. To save her life, they told her, she must sacrifice to the old gods.

A priest was summoned to her household; he refused, how-ever, to perform the ancient ritual in Lahaina. He claimed that

Lahaina had too much Christian praying, too much of Jehovah's influence, for the pagan rites to be successful. So Nāhiʻenaʻena and her companions made the excuse that she must visit her lands at a village eight or ten miles south, where the priest had agreed to hold the ceremony. We can partly reconstruct the ritual. A chicken or a pig had to be sacrificed. It should be slaughtered in a suitable place while the priest recited prayers. The setting was probably an open rocky area with the sea not far away, perhaps the site of an old *heiau.* Nāhiʻenaʻena and her attendants were dressed in ancient fashion; the priest chanted the old prayers, his voice tremulous or powerful as the words and rhythm demanded. One wonders what the princess felt as she took part in the ancient rite. Was there a release from her fears about the stolen dress? Did she sense a quiver of the divine power with which her birth had endowed her? "The world above which Nahienaena treads majestically, / Nahienaena issues forth as a chief of the rising sun."[11]

Lord Byron, the naval officer appointed by the British government to return the bodies of Liholiho and Kamāmalu to Hawaiʻi, states that this sacrifice was "the last, and probably will remain the last sacrifice ever made in the islands by order of a high chief."[12]

Her descent into the "dark heart" of the past, as Keōpūolani would have called it, was a brief one for Nāhiʻenaʻena. Before the end of 1824, she appeared again to be a devout Christian, listening to her missionary teachers. We must depend on these men for our information; they recorded what they saw and heard, perhaps more than a little of what they hoped. But in actuality they could discover only fragmentary evidence of how she spent the hours within the walls of her home, among her many attendants; and they understood little of her feelings. William Richards wrote that "the little princess never appeared so well as now." By January 1825 — Liholiho had been gone for more than a year — she was full of religious questions and asked about the apostles and patriarchs named in the scriptures. Richards listened eagerly to the few reports that came to him from Hawaiians in Lahaina. Apparently at the threshold of adolescence, she went through a period of extreme piety. A chiefess told of a women's church meeting and how Nāhiʻenaʻena had led the prayers. The remarks of the chiefess suggest that for Lahaina residents Nāhiʻenaʻena was princess royal, not only in the old way but even in Christian practice. "All her mothers, the old people that were present," the chiefess said, "are unskillful; they know very little about praying. We all greatly loved her prayer." When the wife of Hoapili asked the princess about her faithful attendance at women's prayer meetings, she replied piously (so the record translates): "You have always told me to be strong, to cast off the old way and walk in the straight path. Your husband has always told me so too; and I remember the words of my mother Keopuolani. She told me it was a good thing to learn the new way. She told me to love God and Jesus Christ; to mind the word of God; to mind the instructions of my good teachers; to keep the Sabbath Day and pray to God." She concluded her long statement (whether it was embellished by chiefess or missionary, we don't know): "I remember all these words of my good mother, and I desire to obey them." This was language which Richards and Stewart would be happy to hear. Translated from the Hawaiian in which Nāhiʻenaʻena spoke, it rings with missionary rhetoric; and it suggests how much the princess had learned from her dark-suited New England mentors.[13]

Further evidence of Nāhiʻenaʻena's Christian ardor was recorded in a journal written by a Tahitian convert. His name was Toteta, and he lived in the household of Hoapili. William Richards translated the journal, which either he or Toteta divided into ten short "chapters."[14] The Tahitian understood much that troubled the heart of Nāhiʻenaʻena; he recognized the painful contradictions, the struggle with vacillation, and her heritage of Polynesian tradition. He wrote that in January of 1825 the princess turned to the Lord. During that month she spoke freely of her religious feeling. Such talk, however, disturbed her friends and the members of her household. Nāhiʻenaʻena was the center of their non-Christian devotion; she was a primary reason for clinging to the ways of the Hawaiian past. These friends and servants yearned to go back to the comfortable life, to the "old sports and play, and to the pleasures of this world." They campaigned hard in their efforts to turn the princess away from Christian piety, just as, earlier, members of the household of Keōpūolani had tried to keep her from Christian prayer. They even laughed at the word of God, ridiculed Him and spoke contemptuously of Him. Toteta brings us close to the tensions in the mind of the ten-year-old princess: "The chief gets no rest."

Nāhiʻenaʻena, not yielding to the pressure around her, continued to speak openly of religious experience and to claim that she had "put off her old heart." She confessed that she had wavered from the Christian path, that she had not believed in God and had sacrificed to the old gods. "I once thought," she was quoted as saying, "that the word of God was a very heavy thing, and burdensome to those that carried it, and a thing to make one sick." Now, however, she claimed to have learned to love the word of God.

The most startling, and perhaps the most painful, change in

attitude of the princess revealed in Toteta's journal is her attempt to be humble and meek of heart. He writes: ''She desires to cast off entirely the rehearsing of names; for her rejoicing is not now in names and titles.'' This meant a rejection of
her birthright, of her sacred rank; this signified that she relinquished her pride in the illustrious stream of ancestors, that
she would not listen to the chants which told of her descent
from the gods and the first human beings, which placed her
origin in the origin of the islands themselves, rising out of the
chaos of black night. Toteta comprehended as no Westerner
could just how difficult this act of humility was for the girl — to
give up listening to the genealogical chants which honored her
as god. Furthermore, she would have to abandon the fine display of ritual and procession which surrounded the move-
ments and rhythms of her life. He knew how difficult it was for
her to say, ''Jesus alone; let him be lifted up; let him be exalted.''

With the fervor of an adolescent fanatic, Nāhiʻenaʻena
scolded the people of her retinue for their noisy ways and for
their drunkenness, as if parroting the missionary voices of her
daily life. She issued an order that those who could not read
hymns would not be allowed to enter her house. She drama-
tized her own religious feelings: One midnight she appeared at
the mission house to request a lamp. Richards asked why she
wanted it; she said she wished to go into the church. Startled,
he asked why she wanted to do this. She answered: ''There are
some wicked people in that house of Jehovah, and I wish to
know who they are.'' Richards, in his usual laconic fashion,
does not provide us with any detail about who the people
might have been or whether there were actually people in the
church. He did, however, ask some of her attendants how the
princess knew about night visitors in the house of God. They

said that she was in the habit of rising at midnight and going there to pray. The princess, in her Christian role, had to find a way to sustain the drama of her days.[15]

The people of Lahaina, while Liholiho was away, undertook a long-term project to honor their princess. They commenced the arduous work of fashioning a yellow feather skirt, nine yards long, for Nāhi'ena'ena to wear on the occasion of her brother's triumphal return. A fine netting had first to be woven of *olona* fiber. Then hundreds of birds, probably the *o'o*, had to be plucked of their few yellow feathers. These feathers were then tied to the mesh in small bunches until a smooth, shining texture was achieved. Nāhi'ena'ena knew of the work going on. The image of herself dressed in such a *pā'ū* stirred a fine un-Christian pride in her heart.

One day in March 1825, a prayer meeting was held at the Lahaina mission house; Nāhi'ena'ena was present. At the conclusion, the worshipers left; Nāhi'ena'ena, however, lingered on the porch. Mrs. Richards observed that she stood in ''a very pensive attitude.'' The missionary wife politely invited the girl into the house and called her husband. For the first time in his association with her, Richards talked alone with Nāhi'ena'ena. There were no servants, no maids-in-waiting, no *kāhili* bearers present. The two talked for more than an hour. Richards conversed in his earnest, devoted fashion, attempting to discover ''the true feelings of her heart.'' She openly confessed her sins and spoke of the trip south of Lahaina, taken more than six months earlier, to sacrifice to the old gods. She repeated, as she often did to her mentors, the instructions of her mother that she love God and obey the word of her teachers. Richards listened carefully; then he approached a subject close to his heart: he spoke to her of the Christian need for modesty and humility. "I endeavored in my instruction to make her feel that, in the eye of God, there is no difference between chiefs and their subjects." Nāhiʻenaʻena's response gives us direct access to the ambivalence of her feelings. Richards repeats her words: "I am exceedingly afraid of the feather *pāʻū* that is making for me." She paused a moment, then added, "It is a thing to lift up one's heart."[16]

Ali'i in London

Liholiho and Kamāmalu were 165 days at sea on their way to England.[1] They stopped once, after ninety-four days of sailing, at Rio de Janeiro. Here for the first time they met another monarch, Emperor Pedro I of Brazil. Hearing of their destination, the British consul gave a ball to present them to the important Brazilian and English families. In his account of the travels of the king and queen, Lord Byron states that Liholiho and Kamāmalu impressed the party guests with "their great gentleness and good humor" and with the way in which they adapted themselves to strange customs. Liholiho, in appreciation for the party, presented the consul with a fan and a feather cape. Emperor Pedro feted the Hawaiian monarchs at a court levee. He treated them with great respect and as token gave the king a handsome sword.

In early March 1824, they sailed from Rio to complete their voyage. They reached Portsmouth on May 21. The British government had not been told of their coming; there was no reception. Captain Starbuck, however, honored the king and queen with a twenty-one-gun salute from *L'Aigle*. And he sent a messenger to the shipowners in London informing them of the arrival of his royal cargo. Starbuck then arranged for the Hawaiian king and his suite to travel by carriage to London. One can imagine the curiosity with which Liholiho and Ka-māmalu gazed at the English countryside, green with grasses and trees they had never seen, alive with birds and flowers which must have appeared exotic to their eyes. They entered the great city itself where the buildings rose taller than grass houses, taller than coconut palms—buildings of stone and brick, neatly marked with rows of windows. They heard the clop-clop of horses over cobbled streets and saw multitudes of carriages similar to the one they traveled in, and multitudes of people, many of them clad in styles they had never seen in Hawaiʻi.

By the time they reached London, the Foreign Office knew of the unexpected royal visitors from the South Seas. Appropriate courtesies had been arranged. Liholiho and his suite were assigned apartments as guests of the British Government at Osborne's, a fashionable hotel on Robert Street off Adelphi Terrace. The Honorable Frederick Gerald Byng, brother of a viscount and a Gentleman Usher of the Privy Chamber, was appointed to be their escort and adviser. Byng had the nickname "Poodle." George Canning, minister of foreign affairs, assigned "Poodle" to wait upon the Hawaiian king, whose name was thought by the British to mean "dog of dog." Secretary Canning's little joke made the rounds of the fashionable society of the day, a society which enjoyed mocking everyone and everything that did not belong to its inner circles and which did not conform to its ways.

One of the first jobs of "Poodle" Byng was to provide

suitable clothing for the Hawaiian royalty. On the long voyage to England, they had worn out the clothes tailored for them in Honolulu. Nor were these suitable for the English climate. They shivered from cold in the English weather of May and June 1824. An early caller on the king and queen found them playing cards with Liliha and Boki, and describes their garments. "The ladies were dressed in loose *robes de chambre*, of straw colour tied with rose-coloured strings, and on their heads they wore turbans of feathers of scarlet, blue and yellow." The men wore plain black coats, silk stockings, and shoes. These were hardly the clothes of royalty; nor were they suited to fashionable London of the early nineteenth century. London tailors and seamstresses were called in. By May 23 Liholiho and Kamāmalu and their suite were ready to go out in public.

Their first formal visit was to Westminster Abbey on Whitsunday. During the services, the visiting king and queen were placed in the choir near the dean of Westminster. Liholiho wore a white waistcoat and black coat. His pea-green gloves "were not long enough to conceal his sooty wrists." According to an observer on that Whitsunday, he stood throughout the whole service and "gazed in amazement at the roof." The queen, described as "a tall, fine, masculine figure," was apparently so frightened by the first burst from the organ as to be thrown into extreme agitation; she would have leaped out of the pew, said the observer, "had not her maid-of-honor (an English lady) prevented her by laying hands upon her." After the services, the dean escorted the royal party around the Abbey. When they reached the chapel of Henry VII, Liholiho refused to enter. He would not step upon the tombs of royalty: this was the kind of sacred past he could understand and honor in his own way.

On May 28 the royal couple was introduced to fashionable London. Secretary Canning held a reception at Gloucester Lodge, Northumberland House. There the guests could stare (and Londoners of the period did indeed stare) at the Hawaiians, dark in color and monumental in proportion. Englishmen were not used to queens six feet tall. Two hundred distinguished guests—among them the duke and duchess of Gloucester, Prince Leopold of Belgium, the duke of Wellington, ambassadors and cabinet ministers—gathered to greet King Liholiho and Queen Kamāmalu. Canning escorted the royal couple along the gallery, through the house, and into the garden; on the way he presented them to the assembled dignitaries. A guards regiment band in full uniform played military music, and a "fine collation" was served in the dining room. Miss Mary Berry, a protégée of Horace Walpole, writing about the reception in her journal, described Kamāmalu as "a large black woman more than six feet high and broad in proportion," who was "muffled up in a striped gauze dress with short sleeves, leaving uncovered enormous black arms." Kamāmalu wore also a large gauze turban, fashionable in the period. Miss Berry observed that one of Liholiho's attendants wore a feather helmet and a scarlet and yellow feather cloak over his European clothes. When the queen was escorted past the band, she showed more interest in the red-plumed hats of the musicians than in the music; and Miss Berry with her acerbic pen comments that "she ought to have been pleased to see that the officer's helmet of her court surpassed them as to color."

The secretary's reception launched Liholiho and Kamāmalu into London life. On May 31 they attended a performance of *Pizarro* at Covent Garden Theatre. When they arrived in the royal box, the audience applauded, and Liholiho, who was naturally dignified and had a sense of ceremony, bowed in response. He remained standing while the orchestra played "God Save the King." During the performance, Queen Kamāmalu wept at some of the touching scenes. A newspaper report of the theatre visit, however, sounds a faintly ominous note: "The Queen labored under a slight cold."

The next week or ten days were filled with activity; the royal party attended a performance at the Drury Lane Theatre, visited the British Museum, watched a balloon ascension, called at Chelsea Hospital and the Royal Military Asylum, went to the races at Epsom—they were astonished at the speed of the horses and spoke of them as flying. The climax of the London visit was scheduled for June 21; King George IV had granted an audience. Liholiho would at last be able to meet with his peer, the king whom he had crossed oceans to see, monarch of the country with which his father had attempted to establish ties.

The audience never took place. On June 10 Manuia, the steward of the party, came down with measles. On June 13 the king suddenly became ill while at a Royal Academy Exhibition at Somerset House. Within five or six days the rest of the Hawaiian group had contracted measles. By June 24 Liholiho and Kamāmalu were so seriously ill that King George's physician, Sir Henry Halford, was called in consultation. Kamāmalu's illness was complicated by an infection of the lungs, and her condition became grave. On July 8, when she was obviously in danger, Liholiho was informed. He commanded that he be placed in a wheelchair and taken to her apartment. There he asked to be lifted onto her bed.

The young king and queen, weak with illness, embraced each other. And they wept together. After a while Liholiho

73

dismissed his attendants, and for some time the royal pair was alone. Lord Byron believed that during this time Liholiho and Kamāmalu made their last promises to each other. They agreed that death would not separate them. At five o'clock Liholiho called in his servants and asked to be returned to his own apartment. By six o'clock the queen was dead.

Liliha, who had served her queen with constant devotion during the illness, took charge of Kamāmalu's body. She dressed it in the Hawaiian way with a *pāʻū* reaching from the waist to below the knees; she left the legs and feet bare. The short black hair she adorned with wreaths of flowers and vines. Kamāmalu in death appeared once again the traditional Hawaiian queen. Liholiho then "desired the body might be brought to his apartment and laid on a small bed near him. This being done, he sat looking at it, but neither speaking nor weeping." The medical attendants tried to urge him to let the queen's body be removed; but for a while he did not respond. Then suddenly he signed that it should be taken away. And he ordered the body to be embalmed in fragrant scents. When all was ready, the queen in her coffin lay in state in Boki's room at the hotel. A black satin pall covered the coffin lid, and over it was placed her feather cloak of state and the yellow coronet of feathers. At the head of the coffin stood a tall *kāhili* and at the foot, a table with two lighted candles.

Kamāmalu was taken to St. Martin's Church for temporary entombment; the king had ordered her body returned to Hawaiʻi. He seemed anxious about her safety in the church; when assured of it, he told his suite that he hoped soon to be with her. Both of them, he commanded, were to be returned to his kingdom for final burial.

On July 13 Liholiho's condition suddenly became much

worse. The doctor was hastily summoned. When he entered the king's apartment, Liholiho seized his hand and said in Hawaiian, "I am dying, I know I am dying." He continued through the daylight hours and into the evening to recognize the people around him; the Hawaiians, as they would have done in their island home, attended his bedside, keeping their final watch. Late in the evening he lapsed into a state of semi-consciousness. He began to repeat, again and again, "I shall lose my tongue, I shall lose my tongue." Liliha cradled his head in her arms; Boki and the others affectionately and sorrowfully held his legs and feet. Finally he whispered to them, "Farewell to you all, I am dead, I am happy." He died in Liliha's arms before dawn on July 14. After his death, Liliha had to be carried to her room.

Liholiho lay in state at Osborne's Hotel. Though death had come to him in a distant land, his Hawaiian subjects attempted to re-create the splendor of Hawaiian royalty to honor their king. Frames were erected on which to hang his feather cloaks of many designs. The scarlet, yellow, and black feathers of Hawaiian birds glowed luminously in the London interior, serving as a background of royal splendor for the king's coffin. The floor was strewn with rose petals, candles flamed, and bouquets of flowers added to the brilliant color. The coffin itself was covered with a black silk pall; on it rested Liholiho's sword, his military hat, and feather cloak of state.

Captain Lord Byron, a cousin of the poet, was chosen to transport the royal remains to Hawai'i in H.M.S. *Blonde*. Though Liholiho's venture to London had ended in death, his journey had important consequences for the kingdom. England turned her eyes to Hawai'i; the first British consul was appointed. A letter from Secretary Canning to George IV dated July 14, 1824, indicates reasons for British interest.

Mr. Canning humbly presumes that Your Majesty will not disapprove of
a ship of War being allowed to carry back the Suite of the deceased
Chief, with the remains of himself and his wife, to the Sandwich
Islands: — an Attention perhaps the more advisable as the Governments
both of Russia and the United States of America are known to have their
Eyes upon those Islands: which may ere long become a very important
Station in the trade between the N. W. Coast of America and the China
Seas.[2]

The frigate *Blonde* sailed on September 28, 1824, from
Portsmouth. In its hold lay the coffins of Liholiho and Kamāmalu; on board were the surviving members of the king's
suite. The voyage took seven months. The sorrowful news was
carried to Hawaiʻi some months ahead of the *Blonde* by
whalers. The British ship stopped at Lahaina before pro-
ceeding to Honolulu. On May 4, 1825, Princess Nāhiʻenaʻena,
surrounded by the mourning Hawaiians, waited on the beach
with her stepfather Hoapili and her teacher William Richards.

8

The Boy-King

When on March 9, 1825, word reached Hawai'i that the king and queen were dead, Kalanimoku, the prime minister, immediately dictated a letter to inform Nāhi'ena'ena at Lahaina, the chiefs at Kona and on Kaua'i. The letter was written in the name of Ka'ahumanu but signed by the heir to the throne, Kauikeaouli. The news frightened the missionaries by a prospect of a return to the violent ceremonies of death. They were also afraid that the king's death abroad would create hostility toward the religion of foreigners. But their hard work now reaped rewards. The expression of Hawaiian sorrow was centered in Christian services of worship. Many of the people seemed to have remembered that Keōpūolani, less than two years before, had ordained that there be no violence at her death, and that Liholiho had reinforced her command. A further stabilizing influence was the general acceptance of the Kamehameha dynasty. Liholiho had named Kauikeaouli to be his successor; the Hawaiians were not left without a king.

Thus "the old enormities" were practiced in only a few places in the kingdom.[1]

Who can now know what Nāhiʻenaʻena felt? She was certainly deeply moved; in her short life she had shared several times in the expression of grief which accompanied death. She was a child quickly roused to displays of emotion; she wept readily. She might have been one of those who, in Stewart's words, let their tears fall silently and rapidly. What we do know is that a month after the news had come, and before the arrival of the bodies, she wrote two letters. One was addressed to the prime minister, the other, jointly to the prime minister and Kaʻahumanu. Stewart tells us that the letters were entirely of her own composition and that they were "handsomely written on gilt-edged paper, correctly folded, and sealed with wax." In one of the letters she asks Kalanimoku and Kaʻahumanu to be parents to Kauikeaouli and herself: "It is not good for us to be without parents." She laments that Liholiho will never return to them. She consoles herself with that commonplace of missionary rhetoric, "The word of our true Lord remains, and let us regard it." She concludes with a message for her brother. "Love to you, O Kauikeauli [sic], my brother! Dead is our king at Lonadona; dead also is the sister of us Kamehamalu."[2]

[Perhaps some observation should be made about the words attributed to Nāhiʻenaʻena: the letters she wrote are not extant. The words she spoke, always in Hawaiian, come to us in the translations of the missionaries who rendered them in the language of the Bible, in the solemn and sober tones of their own discourse. They make Nāhiʻenaʻena sound precocious and express a piety that may not have been altogether there, for we know that even in childhood she wavered between piety and chiefly willfulness; doubtless her actual language was more the language of her tender years — that is, imitation of her elders — than the lofty expressions of devotion we find in the translations. In a word, we are faced here with a missionary form of hagiography, an attempt to give Nāhiʻenaʻena a high religious character which, because of her sacred place in the royal hierarchy, might serve as example to the faithful.]

When the *Blonde* reached Lahaina on May 4, 1825, she was becalmed six miles offshore. Canoes were sent out, and throngs of curious islanders, including the chiefs, gathered on the beach to speculate and wait. Richards too, watched. When he saw that a boatload of people had been lowered from the ship, he joined Hoapili, Nāhiʻenaʻena, and the others on the shore. The first returning canoe sped in with a cry, "It's Boki, it's Boki!" Hoapili signaled Richards to follow and strode down the beach to a chair which had been placed for him. Nāhiʻenaʻena ran after them, clutching Richards' arm. "Stay by me," she urged. The missionary stood next to Hoapili, and the princess leaned at his side.

As the ship's boat drew near, the thousands on the shore began to wail for their dead king and queen. When Boki and Liliha stepped onto the sand, the lamentations increased, but the crowd was orderly enough to open a passage through its midst so that the chiefs from afar might approach Hoapili and Nāhiʻenaʻena. Richards recorded the scene: "Hoapili rose from his chair, threw back his head and with a roar which scarcely resembled the human voice, he spread out his arms to receive his daughter Kuini [Liliha]. In an instant all the chiefs present except the one which leaned on my side and all the thousands around set up a screaming which drowned the roaring of the ocean and thus summoned to the scene of grief those who till now had not heard the alarm. The princess, in utter neglect of all their ancient forms, sprang forward and . . . threw herself into the arms of Kuini; and the latter dropped into the sand, while the tears of the little girl were falling on her breast." Hoapili prostrated himself and buried his face in the dust at Boki's feet; the other chiefs quickly followed him, and "for several minutes scoured their sable faces in the sand."

During this moving scene, Richards did not forget his Christian duties. He reminded Nāhiʻenaʻena that it would be well to thank God for the safe arrival. She spoke to Boki and Liliha, who had remained much calmer than the other chiefs. They gave their hands to the missionary. "Where shall we pray?" Boki asked. And Richards, "hoping that it might stop the confusion and noise which . . . prevailed . . . proposed to remove to a neighboring yard. They approved, and as we began to move, the wailing in good measure ceased." Mats were spread for the chiefs and a prayer service was held.[3]

Richards went the next morning to call on Boki and found him with Nāhiʻenaʻena and the other chiefs. They were waiting for the formal visit of Lord Byron. In the official party, Byron brought Robert Dampier, the young artist of his voyage. Dampier writes that Boki met them on the shore and conducted the commander and his party to a "large covered space, which was one of the king's storehouses. Here we found the young Princess, Madame Boki's Father, herself, and several chiefs together with an American Missionary, who acted as an interpreter." Though the artist, when he reached Honolulu, painted a portrait of Nāhiʻenaʻena which shows a serious and appealing girl, he said on first seeing her that she was "not at all pretty." Her face was "disfigured" by a large white mob cap with which Liliha "had shrouded her royal brows." The child-princess occupied the center of the reception room and was surrounded by her attendants. On either side the chiefs reclined on their mats. Dampier was startled by their corpulence, which showed the effects of their indulgence, as he put it, "with a suitable addition of Pig and Poi."[4]

When the *Blonde* sailed from Lahaina, she carried the princess and the Maui chiefs. In Honolulu, the boy-king, Ka'ahumanu, Kalanimoku and the other nobles awaited the ship's arrival. Opposite the fort, the ship dropped anchor and fired a salute. Thousands of commoners thronged to the beach, held at an appropriate distance by a file of armed men. The chiefs, clad in black, gathered at Ka'ahumanu's house near the quay. A great hush settled over the scene. As the barges from the *Blonde* drew near, Ka'ahumanu, her sisters, and the young queens of Liholiho left the company of chiefs, stepped slowly and silently onto the quay and formed a line. When at last Boki and Liliha could be recognized, the young queens let out a quick cry of grief; this signaled a prolonged wail from the gathered people. But the queens remained quietly in their line. The Maui chiefs, disembarking, drew themselves into a solemn line facing the waiting women. Neither line moved. The people continued to wail; minute guns fired salute after salute. Suddenly, as if from an invisible sign, the two lines of chiefs "rushed into each others' embrace, passing from the arms of one another in a continual paroxysm of weeping." This ceremony of grief continued for an hour until Liliha "at last sunk to the ground from exhaustion, and was under the necessity of being assisted into the house."[5]

Lord Byron did not disembark from the *Blonde* until the following day, when he made his formal call upon the chiefs. Kalanimoku decided to hold the audience, not in his Western style house, but in his new grass house. It is possible that at this moment of national mourning, on the occasion of the re-

turn of the dead son and daughter of Kamehameha I, he
wished to meet the Europeans in the kind of dwelling honored
by generations of chiefs. The reception was almost totally Hawaiian except for the dress; the chiefs chose to wear Western-
style mourning clothes. They wanted Nāhiʻenaʻena, however,
to wear the magnificent yellow feather *pāʻū* lined in crimson
satin — the one which, during its making, had "lifted up her
heart." On her head she was asked to wear the feather coronet
of a Hawaiian princess and around her neck, feather leis. The
little girl, at this moment of sorrow and destiny, was their symbol of ancient tradition, of a past which could not be torn from
their hearts. Nāhiʻenaʻena startled them, however. She spoke
as with the voice of a Puritan, in reality an echo of her dead
mother. If she wore the *pāʻū*, she would be naked above the
waist: and this, she said, was now forbidden. The chiefs attempted to persuade her, but her mission training exacted its
discipline. The girl was for a while frozen in conflict. Then she
burst into hysterical tears and fled to the mission house. Her
Christian teachers had difficulty quieting her. When she
returned to the assemblage, she was wearing a black dress in
the European style.

Lord Byron, his officers, and his scientists landed to a salute
of guns. Boki escorted them to Kalanimoku's house where the
chiefs waited. Kauikeaouli and Nāhiʻenaʻena were seated in
the place of honor upon a Chinese sofa which stood on a platform covered with finely woven mats. Behind them rose four
giant *kāhili* of state. The feather *pāʻū* was spread over Nāhi-
ʻenaʻena's lap and draped on the sofa between the royal children. The chiefs sat according to rank on either side, Kaʻahumanu and the other chiefesses near the princess, and Kalanimoku on a large red chair near the young king. Chairs were arranged for the party from the *Blonde* and for the missionaries.

When Lord Byron and his suite moved into the audience chamber, the chiefs rose; Kauikeaouli, Nāhiʻenaʻena, and Kalanimoku, however, remained seated. After the formal introductions, Lord Byron presented the greetings of the king of England and expressions of condolence on the deaths of Liholiho and Kamāmalu. He then delivered gifts to the high chiefs: a gold hunting watch to Kalanimoku, a wax figure of her late husband to Kīnaʻu; to Kaʻahumanu, an elegant silver teapot engraved with her name and the royal arms of Britain. For Kauikeaouli he had brought a blue Windsor uniform; the gold buttons were engraved with the insignia of the British king: GR. At Lord Byron's suggestion, the boy put on the coat, sword, and hat. The commander then "playfully presented" him to Kaʻahumanu and Kalanimoku as their king. He put his hand on Kauikeaouli's head and "bade him to be a good boy, attend well to his studies, and mind all his kind friends the missionaries said to him."[6]

The twenty-five-year-old Dampier was not impressed by what he saw that day. He complained that the young king had an ugly skin infection, that the chiefs had "hideous faces and misshapen corpulent bodies." The artist's eyes did not discern in the Hawaiians what his illustrious countryman Captain Cook had seen. Dampier's attitude would change, however, on closer acquaintance. He admitted that the funeral of the king and queen was a magnificent spectacle. He further modified what he had earlier said of Nāhiʻenaʻena. After she began to sit for her portrait, he wrote: "The little Princess sat uncommonly well, and I was enabled to make a very good beginning, with which she seemed highly gratified. She is a very well behaved little girl tho' somewhat plain." After two or three weeks of residence, the artist spoke of the fine forms and the beauty of skin color among the Sandwich Islanders.[7]

About a month after the funeral, the chiefs gathered in
council to complete the formalities of Kauikeaouli's accession
to the throne. They invited Lord Byron, Richard Charlton (the
first British consul), the missionaries, and merchants to attend. It was the first time that Western, Christian customs and
attitudes entered into the political process for the declaration
of a new king. The boy was placed under the special guardianship of Kalanimoku; nevertheless, the missionaries were to
continue to instruct him in letters and religion. The powerful
and imperious Kaʻahumanu, *kuhina-nui*, remained as regent
at the center of control. The young king, unlike his brother
(who, robed in a gleaming feather cloak, had walked out on the
beach in Kailua to be acknowledged by the chiefs), responded
to the announcement of his accession in Western rhetoric, just
faintly shaped by the old manner of address. "Where are you,
chiefs, guardians, commoners! I greet you. Hear what I say!
My kingdom I give to God. The righteous chief shall be my
chief, the children of the commoners who do right shall be my
people, my kingdom shall be one of letters."[8]

9
Child of God

At the beginning of Kauikeaouli's reign, the trend toward Christian piety increased. Even the austere and formidable Ka'ahumanu — whose face Dampier described as lowering and having a "peculiar savage and stern look," — accepted missionary teaching. She and Kalanimoku were admitted to membership in the church in December 1825. They attempted to guide the young king, who already manifested chiefly willfulness and a love of pleasure, toward Christian ways; and they directed the nation itself toward Christian conceptions of law and justice. Nāhi'ena'ena became increasingly pious and modest. A speech recorded by Kamakau shortly after Kauikeaouli's accession reveals the shaping influence of her missionary mentors at this time. In the last paragraph she states: "My heart is yearning to trust in Jesus, my Lord and Savior. I pray God to turn all the commoners and chiefs to Him. This has been my constant prayer, that God bless our kingdom, and that the nation as a whole be purified so that the devil may be without power over this nation." The historian comments that the "surprising thing is that in the prayer of this young ruler she placed the commoners first and the chiefs second." It is interesting, too, to observe that Kamakau calls her a "ruler."[1]

Late in December 1825, Kauikeaouli decided to visit Lahaina. There was no announced reason—the whim of a young king, probably, and the ancestral desire to move from place to place; or perhaps the wish for a reunion with Nāhi'ena'ena who had returned to her Maui home after the departure of the *Blonde*. At Lahaina, Kauikeaouli went immediately to his sister's house. Levi Chamberlain, the mission's secular agent in Honolulu and the king's tutor, was present. He states laconically that he witnessed "the meeting of the king with his sister and Hoapili." This is all we know of Kauikeaouli's stay in Lahaina, except Chamberlain's laments about how difficult it was to keep the boy's attention on the serious business of reading and writing, and the fact that the king extended his visit about two months. He and his sister must have been much together. Their parting in February 1826 reveals the tenderness of the love between them.

Chamberlain, apparently moved by what he saw, describes the farewell of the youthful couple. They boarded the ship together, Nāhi'ena'ena's canoes waiting alongside. They did not, however, remain close to each other on deck. The princess, very quiet, very solemn, sat on the railing. Her eyes filled with tears as she watched her brother. Kauikeaouli moved about the ship, delaying the sailing for an hour. Finally Nāhi'ena'ena approached him. But neither seemed to want to look at the other or to speak. Her tears, which had been controlled, began to flood her cheeks. She gave her brother a sideways glance. Then, overwhelmed with feeling, she jumped into a waiting canoe and threw herself into the arms of a favorite attendant; the two sobbed. The king, trying to conceal his emotion, walked away. The ship set sail.[2]

Of the following months, the records are silent about Nāhi-ʻenaʻena. The days at Lahaina came and went in their bright lazy fashion; the indigo shadows of the East Maui Mountains seemed impenetrable, a hidden place for the ancient gods; sun glistened on the beach sand and baked the seagrass. Surf rolled on the shore. Lahaina continued its placid way.

The young nation, however, was struggling with the task of composing a code of law. The old *kapu* system must be supplanted with some pattern of order. Certain foreigners — especially missionaries — wanted to help the Hawaiians legislate for moral order and justice in the diverse population. Others enjoyed the licentious freedom which all too often prevailed. Among these latter were ships' captains and sailors who wanted what they considered their rightful prerogatives of women and spirits ashore. They hated the laws established by the chiefs, especially those regulating gambling, prostitution, and the sale of rum. In Honolulu and Lahaina, regular ports of call, the sailors protested against the new regulations. In 1825 sailors rioted in Lahaina and laid seige to Richards' house. Again in 1827 another riot was threatened by the unscrupulous British consul. He sent a message warning the chiefs to take Nāhiʻenaʻena to a safe place. Thus the girl, even in indirect fashion, was caught in political — and what might be called international — pressures. Certainly the chiefs and attendants in her large household talked endlessly, Hawaiian fashion, about all they could hear of the news. The princess listened to their chatter, perhaps wondering at her own role in changing events.

At times during the years 1826 and 1827, Nāhiʻenaʻena

visited Honolulu. In December 1826, when Kalanimoku fell seriously ill, the chiefs were summoned to his bedside. During this visit the princess appears to have been the pious Christian her teachers had worked with Puritan determination to create; they planned that this royal child might become the salvation of the nation. She went regularly to chapel and prayer. When she heard that her brother was indulging himself (probably gambling), she prevailed upon him to go to the home of Christian Kaʻahumanu.[3]

In 1825 Nāhiʻenaʻena had told Richards that she planned to give herself to God; she was about ten years old. The ceremonial climax of her religious ardor came two years later, in January 1827, when she was admitted to the church. The church records at Lahaina describe the state of her mind during this period. She appeared to be a "child of God" and showed "stability of Christian character." Consequently, the missionaries decided she should be "folded in the arms of the church and guarded as a lamb of the flock." They selected the date carefully so that the ceremony might have political overtones. Kalanimoku's health had continued to decline, and in January 1827 he decided to return to his home in Kona to die. On the way, the "Iron Cable of Hawaii" would stop on Maui to make his last visit to Lahaina. Seizing this propitious moment, the missionaries scheduled two important events: a celebration of the Lord's Supper for the ailing Christian prime minister; and the ceremony during which Nāhiʻenaʻena, the wife of Hoapili, and several others would be baptized. Each of the candidates had already been thoroughly prepared, each had been questioned in private about his state of mind. Each must now make a public statement of faith in the presence of the congregation during the baptismal ceremony. On that im-

portant occasion, Richards queried Nāhiʻenaʻena. Her recorded answer was: ''Since the first time that I told you that I had
given myself away to the Lord, I have had but one thought,
and that is that as I have set out I cannot go back; and if all the
other chiefs adhere to the old system, still I have but one
thought, and that is to follow the Lord though it be alone.''
After all candidates had pledged themselves, the articles of
faith were read. And Nāhiʻenaʻena was at last ''sprinkled with
water'' in the name of God. She took the baptismal names of
her mother, Keōpūolani and Harieta.[4]

In 1827 a British officer threatened to destroy Lahaina.
This was at the time that the British consul, Richard Charlton,
had sent word that the chiefs should take Nāhiʻenaʻena to a
safe place. In his journal Chamberlain records that Nāhiʻena-
ʻena had told Richards that a ship's captain had bought a Hawaiian woman for $160.00. When in November of 1827 Boki,
governor of Oʻahu, was told of the princess' statement, he
remarked, ''*wahaheʻe*,'' liar.
    In that same month Nāhiʻenaʻena and the chiefs were sum-
moned by Kaʻahumanu to Honolulu for a council to discuss
business of the nation and the problems of the missions vis à
vis the angry and rioting seamen. On November 26, 1827,
Richards was invited to the council to answer charges of mis-
conduct. The charges against him centered on the statement
of the purchase of the woman, a statement which had reached
the newspapers of the United States. During the council, Boki
read a *manaʻo*, an opinion, from King Kauikeaouli and
Princess Nāhiʻenaʻena. They stated that they would take steps
to prevent any violence against Richards. They would, however, condemn the person who had committed the wrong. ''If
Mr. Richards should be found to be wrong he should be sent to

his own country, if in the right he should be justified and approved."

A day or so later the council of chiefs dismissed the charges against Richards and moved their discussion to the more difficult problems of their nation: the relationship with Great Britain and the drafting of moral laws. When the council ended, laws against murder, theft, and adultery had been promulgated.[5]

During this visit of Nāhiʻenaʻena to Honolulu, the king held a horse race—one of his favorite pastimes. Before the race started, the princess was seen riding with the unprincipled British consul toward the racing ground. The missionaries were worried about their "lamb of God." They waited. In a short while, however, the princess returned and was present at evening prayer. There is no evidence that the more serious gossip of Honolulu during those months of November and December reached the mission houses. Tongues wagged in the capitol that the king and his sister were sleeping together and planned to marry.[6]

Part II

10

"Where the Lava Gathered"

In a romance, Nāhiʻenaʻena would be the beautiful and tragic Hawaiian princess separated from her beloved brother by blind and bumbling men from the Western world who could not understand the harmonious structure of her traditional culture. She could become another image of that pure spirit — the Noble Savage — corrupted by American or European forces, by "civilization" entering and ravaging the islands of the Pacific. And if she were a princess in a fairy tale, a drink from a magic philter, the wave of a wand, the touch of a talisman would restore her happiness and her power. She would become once again the sacred daughter on her mythic island.

She was, instead, a flesh-and-blood girl who lived in an archipelago remote and unknown to most of the Western world. And she lived at a time when, because of the adventurous and greedy spirit of man, these two worlds were being brought together. Her own adventurous, land-seeking ancestors had long ago voyaged in canoes across the blue reaches of the Pacific.

Heiress of the Polynesian past, heiress to her father's and her race's hunger for the new, she was caught in the contradictions of her double heritage.

Nāhiʻenaʻena was a princess royal in love with her brother. Nāhiʻenaʻena was (at times) a pious Christian girl, brought up to live "like a missionary wife." How could such roles harmonize within the consciousness of a young woman? Perhaps if she and her brother had been lesser chiefs—not so much at the traditional and dynastic center of the nation—she might have managed a dual life as had other chiefesses of her time.

The missionaries had reached her when she was young enough to be shaped to some of their patterns and to have her sensibility touched by the mysteries of a new religion. They understood the importance of her person; they recognized her as an instrument of power. These men of God had remained close to her during the last illness of her mother, whom they had "saved" by their persuasiveness and their visions of hellfire. Keōpūolani too had molded her small daughter. She had defied ancient custom to retain the child at her side so that she might oversee her rearing. Nāhiʻenaʻena was proud in later years to sign her letters Keōpūolani. The sacred wife of Kamehameha had set the stage on which her daughter's short life was played out: she had imbued the child with an inner sense of her supreme worth as a Hawaiian *aliʻi*, a regal figure in the nation, and as a Christian. But Keōpūolani had not been a Christian long enough to recognize how much of the old must be relinquished, how in missionary eyes a man must be totally a Puritan Christian. She did not realize how much of the old culture would be regarded as evil and the work of the devil.

Nāhiʻenaʻena, however, did learn. She was taught the many wickednesses of the old "dark heart." She was taught about sin and what would happen if she performed sinful acts. To dance, to listen to the old chants, play the old games, drink wine, play cards: these were evil. The major evil was to love her brother with physical passion. She realized that she was retained in Lahaina by Hoapili and Richards to keep her from the revelry of the court in Honolulu, but most of all to separate her from Kauikeaouli.

So the two towns, Lahaina and Honolulu, became symbols of ways of life. Lahaina was home; it was the place of learning, the place of residence of her teachers Stewart (who left in 1825) and Richards, both of whom were like fathers to her: it was where her mother was buried. In Lahaina life was good — and boring. Honolulu was the center of wickedness — gambling, adultery, dancing, drinking wine and rum, the corrupting influence of dissolute foreigners. It was a place where the devil remained close at her shoulder; it was also a place of delight. She resided in Lahaina. Kauikeaouli, the brother-king resided in Honolulu.

The royal boy and girl, however, could not be kept forever apart. Nāhi'ena'ena was summoned to Honolulu if a great chief fell ill, or for the councils of the nation and other state events. The young king, who unlike his sister had never been touched deeply by missionary training, and who followed his own pleasure-bent, willful ways, traveled a good deal, not only on O'ahu but among the islands of his kingdom. From time to time he went to Lahaina.

An episode, for which there are scant details, reveals how the royal children continued to be rooted in the mythical ground of their race. It suggests how, in spite of political and social changes brought about within less than ten years after the death of Kamehameha I, his sacred son and daughter

95

could still pursue their own desires, visit the places of the old gods. Missionaries and disapproving chiefs could not always separate the chiefs destined to be joined together. "When the chiefs are joined," so runs the chant, "the earth is eternal."

In mid-1828, the king sailed to Lahaina on his warship *Kamehameha*. He had with him, in addition to Boki and other attendant chiefs, a flamboyant and dissolute group of young men and courtiers called the Hulumanu, bird feathers; the full significance of their name, birds of foul feathers, was appropriate for a group that spent its time and substance on women, rum, and gambling. The Hulumanu and their leader, an unscrupulous Tahitian called Kaomi, had considerable influence on Kauikeaouli, who enjoyed their licentiousness and drunkenness. The arrival of the *Kamehameha* and its escort vessels ruffled the serene and pious days of Lahaina. Nāhiʻenaʻena, however, rejoiced to see her brother and to be with him; she, Hoapili, and the other chiefs feasted the king and his suite.[1]

The king's plan was not simply to visit Maui; he had set out to view Kīlauea Volcano on the island of Hawaiʻi. And he wanted his sister to accompany him. Thus, when he left Lahaina, he took Nāhiʻenaʻena with him. The royal pair had never seen the volcano, though it is located on the island of their birth. They had never gazed into the pit at the fires of Pele, the goddess who had made the migratory voyage—as, traditionally, had the first Hawaiians—from Bora Bora. According to the old chant, "From Kahiki came the woman, Pele,/ From the land of Pola-pola." It tells how Pele yearned for Hawaiʻi and carved the canoe for the voyage.[2] Kauikeaouli and Nāhiʻenaʻena traveled not only to view a famous phenomenon and visit the domain of the fire goddess; on this trip they also returned to the island of their origin, where for a few years they had lived within the tradition of their ancestors. Although they did not plan to go to Kailua or Keauhou (Kauikeaouli had been in Kona in April) they must have had memories and feelings—for Hawaiians hold place in special regard. The trees and foliage, the flowers and grasses, the rock and shape of land, the sea, the rain and sun of places where they have lived or spent time are charged with psychic intimacy. In nuance and emotion, old *mele* and chants reveal this involvement with place.

At Hilo, the reception of the king was not cordial. Kamakau chronicles that the chiefs did not offer their lands, as was the custom, but only cooked foods. Boki, in an attempt to restore the king's dignity and prerogative, gave him his lands in the district of Hilo to distribute. This action only further irritated the Hilo chiefs. Kauikeaouli and Nāhi'ena'ena set off quickly for the volcano and its fires.[3]

Charles Stewart, before his departure from Hawai'i three years earlier, had visited with Lord Byron the crater of Kīlauea and had left a description of the journey from Hilo. For the first four miles out of Hilo, he wrote, the traveler moved through open stretches of land shaded at intervals by clumps of breadfruit, pandanus, or *kukui* (candlenut) trees. Then the trail entered a wood, where the trees were "hung in luxuriant festoons and pendants" of vines. The wood became increasingly dense, impenetrable in places—a rain forest— and the terrain underfoot was jagged and treacherous, pitted or clinkery with old lava flows. In occasional open areas in the forest, the traveler could view the slow-rising flanks of the great mountains, Mauna Kea and Mauna Loa. For Stewart and Byron, the journey from Hilo to the crater—about thirty miles—took two days.

We do not know precisely how long it took the king and his

sister. They had the advantage of a train of attendant chiefs
and servants to make their journey comfortable. Outriders
traveled ahead to construct bowers of fresh branches to provide accommodation for rest or for sleep at night. The people
living in the forested area brought gifts of food and flowers. At
Kīlauea crater, we may imagine, the young couple descended
into the huge amphitheater of rock and walked across the
black lava to view the firepit. Here and there sulfurous steam
spurted or drifted out from cracks; an occasional fern unrolled
its fronds in a sheltered place. At the edge of the firepit, servants spread mats for the brother and sister. They watched the
red fountaining of lava, its flaming streams, heard the hollow
roar as of surf on the reef. The black and red, constantly
metamorphosing shapes of lava fascinate and mesmerize.
Stewart, often the romantic, writes extravagantly of looking into a "black and horrid gulf not less than eight miles in cir-
cumference" and of "the hideous immensity" to which were
added "the muttering and sighing, the groaning and blow-
ing" of the lava. Then in a more subdued tone he says that "it
was sufficient employment for the afternoon, simply to sit and
gaze at the scene."[4]

It is difficult to imagine that the king and his sister would
gaze at molten lava for an afternoon. The trip had unexplored
and undefined meanings for them. A small detail suggests a
dimension. A black man had vowed to leave his hair at the
edge of the crater in Pele's keeping. He had preceded the
royal party by two days, and after making his offering he
joined the retinue of Kauikeaouli.[5] For him, as for others, the
fire goddess was not a forbidden deity.

But Pele retained her grip upon the Hawaiian imagination,
and would continue to. She was said to appear in many forms:
an ancient wrinkled hag, a seductive young woman, a frighten-

ing divine creature riding in a chariot of flame. Her nature
was as tempestuous as her lava, riven by passion, jealousy,
desire for vengeance, lust for power. Her hula was sacred; it
was often performed on solemn occasions to honor kings and
high chiefs. Her place, the volcano, exhaled, along with its lava
and fire and fume, ancestral memories. Liholiho's abrogation
of the gods eight years earlier could not destroy the fire goddess, just as it could not destroy the molten lava.[6]

Another recorded fragment indirectly suggests the perva-
sive influence of Pele throughout this journey, and in particular the linking of volcanic fire and Nāhiʻenaʻena's name. John
Papa Iʻi, who made the trip with the princess and the king,
alluded to it thirty years later in his notes on history. He told
of a visit to Kīlauea crater long after Nāhiʻenaʻena's death.
"When they went down into the hollow of the pit and came to
the crater proper, which was active, it seemed to Ii that . . .
Nahienaena [was] also there, sitting . . . on the other side
where the lava gathered." Nāhiʻenaʻena, raging fires; and
Pele, goddess of fire: images haunted the mind of the historian.[7]

Kauikeaouli escorted his sister back to Lahaina before his
return to Honolulu. Two newly arrived Americans were there
at the time. They were Dr. and Mrs. Gerrit P. Judd who had
come in March 1828 with the third group of missionaries. Mrs.
Judd, a spirited young woman, described in her journal the
young king and his sister. Kauikeaouli, she said, was "dressed
like a midshipman, in a blue jacket and white pantaloons, and
a straw hat." The king noticed that the mission doctor's wife
wore a dress of red and brown, and promptly sent one of his
servants to make a lei of flame-colored flowers to match it. "I
felt obliged to wear it at dinner, although it was not to my
taste, for I had given away all my muslins, ribbons, and em-

broideries when I became a missionary." Of Nāhiʻenaʻena she
wrote simply and directly: "The young princess, Nahienaena,
is more sprightly than her royal brother. They both have ex-
cellent voices and are patrons of large singing schools." Mrs.
Judd saw the boy and girl in their Lahaina, missionary role.[8]

There were other trips for Nāhiʻenaʻena—good Christian
journeys. She traveled with Richards to the island of Lānaʻi to
examine the schools and churches there. She circled the island
of Maui on a grand tour, taking a retinue with her.[9]
The Maui journey was linked with one made by Richards
and the two new men of God stationed on the island, Lorrin
Andrews and Jonathan Green. The three missionaries had a
dual purpose: one, to visit schools and churches, and the other,
to see the island itself. In a long account of their journey, they
said they wanted to see "the length and breadth of the land—
to ascend its lofty mountains—cross its fruitful plains, de-
scend into its valleys, to learn the state of the people." They
set out in a double canoe and sailed from Lahaina to Wailuku
around the west and north end of Maui; on the way they stopped at villages to visit the people and examine any schools that
might have been established. The princess, though leaving on
the same day, journeyed by land across the mountains to
Wailuku. The two parties planned a rendezvous there at the
mission.
Wailuku had been important in the chronicle of Nāhiʻena-
ʻena's mother and father. There, Kamehameha in 1790 had
fought a bloody battle, and there, Keōpūolani while still a girl
had fled from the army of her future husband across the
mountains to Olowalu, near Lahaina. In 1828 their young
daughter was evidence of the great change in Hawaiʻi; she had
the manner of an exemplary Christian. The showpiece, the

royal pupil who demonstrated the grace and benefit of Western schooling, she delivered a public speech for the Wailuku mission. "On such occasions," the missionaries wrote, "she appeared with a good degree of dignity and her addresses were appropriate."

The princess and the men of God were not always received with warmth and largesse on the Maui trip. In a district beyond Wailuku, the Hawaiians had not yet turned to Christian ways. They were indifferent to the missionaries—and to Nāhiʻenaʻena, who spoke as with their voice. "It was no small difficulty that the people could be induced to listen to the Princess."

After leaving this unfriendly spot, Nāhiʻenaʻena continued her tour along the shore. But Richards and his associates wanted to climb the mountain Haleakalā. The men were eager to see the beauty of this immense extinct crater. At the top, they gazed into the desert of cinder cones and at earth colored in delicate reds, browns, purples, blues by the action of ancient fires. If the day was not misty, they saw across the crater the break of Kaupō Gap where once the lava had pushed through the mountain wall and spilled down the long slope into the sea; and, if the weather held, they had a glimpse across the channel of Mauna Kea and Mauna Loa on the island of Hawaiʻi.

After this diversion they rejoined the princess on the coast, and the two parties traveled together visiting schools and churches. At Honomū, the princess decided to stop for a rest. But the missionaries wanted to move on; they complained that Nāhiʻenaʻena dallied too much along the way. They were single-minded in their travels; the princess had other desires. So they went on to Wailua by canoe, while the princess enjoyed herself. The two parties met again at Kaupō. A large

school had been established there to take care of the people of
that vast and scattered district. It was a remote place where
life was hard because of the lava desert where little rain fell. In
Kaupō's bleak and powerful landscape, the huge mountain
and the glittering sea dominate, and man seems but a small
creature attempting to cope with desolation. In spite of the
school and the energies of the mission, the people were still
frightened of the *palapala*, learning and Scriptures. They
gathered, however, to hear their princess speak. She reminded
them of the Hawaiʻi of the past—of the power of the chiefs
and the powerlessness of the commoners. She spoke of the
Hawaiʻi of the present, which was tempered with the word of
God. Richards records some of her words. "Formerly we [the
chiefs] were the terror of the country—when visiting your district—we should perhaps have bidden you erect a heiau, and
after being worn out with this labour, we should have sacrificed you in it. Now we bring you the *palapala*—the word of
God—why should you fear it?" These words, according to
Richards, were her own. And they probably were. At about
thirteen, she manifested some of the willfulness and the sense
of power typical of a traditional chiefess. Richards, perhaps
naïvely, was delighted with the accomplishment of his pupil.

The journey commenced again, and they traveled along the
southern coast of Maui and up the western shore to Kīhei. At
this village the princess, in a regal gesture, invited the missionaries to take seats in her large canoe for the journey home.
Back in Lahaina, the men of God recorded with customary ex-
actitude that the excursion had taken eleven days and eight
hours.[10]

About ten days before starting on the journey around the
island, Richards had had reason to be disturbed. Two men had

called on him. They brought news that two retainers from the princess' household had waited on the king during his visit with the Hulumanu in Lahaina. The two importuned Kauikeaouli to "sleep with his sister." The king refused. They would not accept his rebuff and continued to urge him. The king remarked that if he did such a thing he would be considered a criminal by all. The princess' men insisted he need not be troubled by such considerations. "Do you go and sleep with your sister." Kauikeaouli, irritated by their persistence, moved away from them to sit near Boki and other chiefs attendant upon him. Who the men were and what their ultimate purpose was we do not know. The missionaries were reminded, however, of the dangerous possibility that a marriage between brother and sister might still take place.[11]

In late November 1828, the princess was summoned to Honolulu. Kauikeaouli, who had been leading a life of uncurbed pleasure—horse racing, gambling, bowling, drinking—had developed an ugly swelling on his neck. It was so painful that he could not sleep at night, and the chiefs gathered around their monarch in the old way to comfort him. The swelling did not heal, and their concern deepened; they ordered the *Kamehameha* to Lahaina to bring the chiefs to Honolulu. Nāhi'ena'ena, her retinue, and the wife of Hoapili returned aboard the brig, reaching Honolulu on December 6.

The *Kamehameha* also brought a letter to Chamberlain from Richards, who was worried about the princess' trip to Honolulu. He feared that she would be "greatly exposed to temptation," and he asked the mission's fiscal agent to watch over the girl. Such concern could not have been stimulated by gossip alone; he must have had other evidence. His earlier confidence in his royal pupil seemed to be wavering: he could not be as certain of the words he had once written in the Lahaina church records: "[She] manifested . . . a stability of Christian character."

Chamberlain responded promptly to the plea. On December 8, the day he received the letter, he called on Nāhiʻenaʻena, who was living at the house of the king. He found the brother and sister together; Kauikeaouli reclined on a mat, and the princess sat by his side. Chamberlain asked courteously about the king's health, and Kauikeaouli answered that he was fully recovered. In the account to Richards, Chamberlain wrote that the princess "seemed to be pleased to see me." When he rose to take his leave, she accompanied him. At his house, "she tarried some time, went into the printing office and walked into my room." After her visit to Chamberlain, she called on the Binghams and stayed with them into the evening. Nāhiʻenaʻena, in her usual fashion, was following the impulses of her nature. The missionaries were solicitous, and so she was friendly. She reached out to them; yet she could return to her brother's house. In Honolulu, her double life, a conflict in Lahaina, could be acted out.

In spite of her friendliness and seeming desire to seek mission companionship, Chamberlain was uneasy. What he had seen at the king's house was innocent enough. But he knew only too well the dissolute life which the young king had established; and in his household Nāhiʻenaʻena was at the heart of it. Richards had warned Chamberlain of the great temptations to the cherished pupil. Thus, a week after his call, he invited the chiefs to tea. Boki and Kauikeaouli declined. Their excuse was the king's illness. "I might perhaps say pretended illness," Chamberlain set down in his journal. Two days later the king, his sister, and other chiefs were summoned to Lahaina; Hoapili was ill. Before sailing, Nāhiʻenaʻena and Hoapili's

wife called on Chamberlain "to give us their aloha. I wrote a
hasty note to Mr. Richards."

After the royal departure, a ship's captain informed Hiram
Bingham that there was much talk of the king's marrying his
sister. The captain had his information from the British consul, Charlton, who, he said, claimed that he did not approve of
such action but was unwilling to take any steps to prevent it; if
he did, the missionaries would accuse him of trying to en-
courage it. Charlton stated flatly that "the king and his sister
slept together every night."

When Chamberlain learned this, he decided he must discover the truth. He had a source he felt he could rely on: the
chiefess Namahana, a former wife of Kamehameha I and sister
to Ka'ahumanu. She was a devout Christian with a warm
heart, but she was a person of political power. She was formidable not only politically; she was immense—more than six
feet tall and very fat. She took pride in the vast quantities of
food she could eat.

Namahana lived in a neatly painted, two-story house of
wood, with a balcony and large windows. When Chamberlain
called, Namahana probably rested comfortably on her mats,
her accustomed position, while servants waited to attend her
or roll her over when she needed to shift her weight. Though
Chamberlain writes of his visit with greater length than usual,
it still is little more than a skeleton of the incident. He had apparently planned his strategy: He did not immediately make
known the purpose of his call. He first asked when Namahana
expected the chiefs and the king to return to Honolulu. She
answered that the chiefs would return as soon as Hoapili was
well enough. Chamberlain asked if the king would come back
with them. No, the chiefess said. The missionary then edged

105

toward the purpose of his visit. He asked if the king planned to remain long in Lahaina. Namahana replied that he wanted to visit the island of Hawaiʻi. Chamberlain then asked about the princess. Would she accompany her brother? Probably not, the chiefess replied. Chamberlain shifted his ground. He asked if the chiefs had decided upon a wife for the king. Namahana said that they very much wanted him to marry. Who? the missionary asked. The daughter of Kuakini, a girl named Manele, "but it is not certain the king will fancy her." The missionary pressed; he asked what the chiefs thought about the king's marrying his sister. Namahana replied that the chiefs did not approve, though some commoners wanted it. "Does Boki favor it?" She answered without confidence, "ʻae paha" [yes, maybe].

Chamberlain finally approached the reason for his visit. "I then asked what was Nāhiʻenaʻena's conduct while she was here on her recent visit. She replied, 'It was very good.' I then said it has been reported by a certain foreigner that the king slept with her every night—she said, *wahahee* [liar]. I continued, the same foreigner says the chiefs are desirous that the king should marry his sister—her answer was *palau* [exaggeration]."

Chamberlain, blunt and single-minded, finally questioned Namahana about where the king and his sister had slept when they were together in the house at night. The chiefess answered specifically. Kauikeaouli slept in one place and Nāhiʻenaʻena in another. Chamberlain asked, did Namahana know this to be true? "Yes, I and several other females lay between them and they did not come together. In the daytime they lay on the mat but at night they slept apart." Chamberlain ends his little matter-of-fact chronicle: "This is just as I supposed."[12]

11

"Thus It Is Continually"

During the next three or four years, Nāhiʻenaʻena moved in the complicated design of a dance, one that might have been the creation of Pele herself. It was choreographed with dignified state appearances and humble acts of piety; it was agitated by arrogant and angry sallies, by impulses of passion and remembrances of lost power; it was tempered by withdrawals, some sullen, some filled with remorse and overtures of kindness. She danced out the zigzag of her "double-bind."

The kingdom too was troubled and conflicted. More and more Western attitudes and practices were introduced. Hawaiians yearned for the bright clothes, the rum, the sophisticated European ways; most of them rejected the somber, stern modes of the men of God. The chiefs struggled among themselves for control, drawing for support on both Western and traditional culture—whichever might work. The young Kauikeaouli remained in his minority the titular king. He was indulged; and his royal will was often tempestuous. In the minds of some chiefs, however, he had a rival in the infant son of his half-sister Kīnaʻu, another daughter of Kamehameha. Certain of the chiefs schemed, manipulating for power. Boki—a restless, ambitious, impulsive man, and governor of Oʻahu—wanted to destroy the dominance of the formidable Kaʻahumanu; he also wanted Kauikeaouli to remain on the throne. This mercurial chief was never able in any of his machinations to plan carefully and at long range; he kindled quickly to situations of the moment. In one of his abortive attempts to oust Kaʻahumanu, he involved Nāhiʻenaʻena.

In June 1829 the princess went to Honolulu. Boki met her. He was drunk: he blustered that she should kill Kaʻahumanu and her family; then she should marry her brother or, as Chamberlain recorded his argument, "You will not be king of these islands." He became increasingly menacing and stated that if she did not marry her brother and have a "rightful heir to the kingdom," Kaʻahumanu would place Kīnaʻu's son on the throne. The princess—nearly a grown young woman at fourteen—told Boki he was foolish. The drunken chief seized the sacred chiefess by an ear and pulled her along as if she were an ordinary person. He fulminated: "What did you come down here for; did you come down as a god to be worshipped?" He tried to drag her to the house of the king. But two chiefesses of her retinue intervened, and attendants ran off to inform the wife of Hoapili. Nāhiʻenaʻena pulled herself away from the hands of Boki and went to the house of other chiefs.

Kaʻahumanu was resting at her quiet retreat in Mānoa Valley at the time. When she heard of Boki's behavior, she hastened back to Honolulu. Her presence apparently calmed the situation. In another one of his abortive sallies for power, the governor had been thwarted. Excitement in the village of Honolulu subsided, and Kaʻahumanu and Nāhiʻenaʻena took tea at the Binghams' in the evening.

108

The next afternoon the Chamberlains had the chiefs to tea—the king, his sister, Kaʻahumanu, and others. The talk was of Boki. The king reiterated that he wanted Kaʻahumanu to be his *kahu*, his adviser and guardian. Kaʻahumanu reassured the Chamberlains that the king was much improved in behavior, that he seemed to be returning to ways that were righteous and good, the *pono*.[1]

Kauikeaouli's good and righteous conduct lasted at least until July 3, 1829. On that day, the fourth Kawaihaʻo Church was dedicated; and the missionaries recognized that, though God was central to the holy significance of the ceremony, the king and his sister must necessarily be central to the human, political significance. The church, a large thatched structure, had been erected under the auspices of the king and Kaʻahumanu. Thousands of people gathered for the ceremony, crowding inside and outside the new building. The king and his sister sat on a red damask sofa which had been placed in front of the pulpit. The young monarch was dressed in a Windsor uniform and the princess in "a dress becoming her high rank and improved character and taste." Both had been carefully instructed in appropriate behavior for such an occasion. The great chiefs, Kaʻahumanu, Hoapili, Kīnaʻu, and others, were seated close to the royal pair. Near the door, some distance away, were chairs for Boki and his wife Liliha.

To open the ceremony, the king mounted the pulpit. The missionaries had told him how King Solomon had taken part in the dedication of the temple; he must have sensed drama in his own action and prerogative. He spoke simply: "Chiefs, teachers and commons, hear: we have assembled here to dedicate to Jehovah, my God, this house of prayer, which I have built for him. Here let us worship him, listen to the voice of his

109

minister, and obey his word." After this royal opening, the choir sang psalms, the missionaries offered prayers, the dedication sermon based on Psalm 132 was delivered by Reverend Hiram Bingham: "We will go into his tabernacles; / We will worship at his footstool." At the conclusion of the dedication prayer, the princess rose to address the congregation, "presenting a cloud of faces." She acknowledged the supremacy of God and repeated what her brother had said at the opening. She also recalled his words spoken soon after his investiture as king, in which he proclaimed that his people would be the faithful and righteous people of the land. When she was seated, the choir sang the concluding psalm in Hawaiian. Surprising everyone, Kauikeaouli again stood up. *"Epule kakou,"* let us pray, he said. He acknowledged God as his sovereign and confessed that he had sinned; he begged God's mercy, stating that he was in need of pardon and cleansing. And he asked God's blessing on all. The missionaries were delighted with this first genuine display of Christian feeling by Kauikeaouli.

In his chronicle of the dedication ceremony, Bingham writes that Kaʻahumanu regarded the princess "as the future partner of the throne." What did he mean? Certainly not marriage. Was he suggesting that Nāhiʻenaʻena might become the *kuhina-nui* after the death of Kaʻahumanu? Was he implying that her power was already considerable, especially as he notes in the same passage that she was "accustomed openly to counsel their own people [the Hawaiians]"? Whatever the implications of his comment, it suggests that the princess remained a symbol, perhaps a power, to be reckoned with in the kingdom.[2]

After the dedication, Nāhiʻenaʻena returned to Lahaina. Within the month, the missionary Lorrin Andrews wrote to Chamberlain in Honolulu of "unfavorable appearances in the princess." He said that he hoped Richards, upon his return to Maui, would have a good influence on her.[3]

Early in October 1829, Charles Stewart returned to Hawai'i; he had left the mission station in 1825 because of his wife's illness. During the interim he had become a navy chaplain and was assigned to the USS *Vincennes*, Captain Finch, commander. The *Vincennes*, on a tour of the Pacific, called first at Hilo in the Hawaiian chain. Stewart records his anticipation of the landfall—he remembered vividly his first one in 1823 when, as now, he had approached the island of Hawai'i. He was, he said, "restless and feverish in mind, as a child on the point of realizing some long promised and eagerly anticipated delight."[4]

The *Vincennes* remained ten days at Hilo, then sailed to O'ahu, without stopping at Maui. Stewart gazed intently as Diamond Head came into view, the coconut groves of Waikīkī, the broad plain of Honolulu; the landscape "looked as if seared with fire," for the island had suffered a long period of drought. He was pleased with the changes in the village of Honolulu: the new stone quays, the dockyards and storehouses at the waterfront, the Blonde Hotel (owned by Boki), and many buildings constructed in European style. He soon learned that the king had built a new royal establishment on the outskirts of the town, near Punchbowl hill. This compound, surrounded by a sturdy fence, contained buildings for eating, sleeping, and conducting government business. At some distance from them stood the royal audience chamber, or palace, enclosed in a special fence. The palace was a large thatched building erected on a pebbled area—Kauikeaouli still held to some of the old ways.[5]

Captain Finch, Stewart, and the other officers paid a formal call on the king, and Stewart saw how Western customs had come to the court. The royal guard, in white and scarlet uniform, was drawn up before the palace. The general of the king's army stood at the entrance to welcome the honored guests. They entered through elegant folding glass doors into a very different chamber from the one in which Stewart had first met Liholiho. The thatch was screened by stems of mountain vines "of a rich chestnut color" tied to give the appearance of bamboo blinds. The floor was not spread with rushes and mats, but was constructed of polished cement. The furniture was Western — richly upholstered chairs, pier tables, mirrors, chandeliers, ormolu wall brackets. At the center of the room stood the throne, draped with a handsome cloak of yellow feathers. The king in Windsor uniform, "a fine, stout young man of sixteen," awaited them on his throne. Kaʻahumanu and Kīnaʻu were at his right and the other high chiefs nearby. During the ceremonies Captain Finch presented Kauikeaouli with his credentials and a letter of greeting from the president of the United States written over the signature of Samuel Southard, secretary of the navy. Bingham read the letters, translating them into Hawaiian. The formalities over, Captain Finch presented gifts for the king: a pair of globes, one of the earth and the other of the heavens, and a large map of the United States; for Kaʻahumanu, a silver vase inscribed with the "arms of the United States"; and for the princess, two silver goblets similarly inscribed. Nāhiʻenaʻena, however, was in Lahaina.[6]

Stewart wanted more than anything to visit Lahaina, to see the Richards family and his little princess. Thus a day or two after the reception, he called on Kaʻahumanu to ask for help in getting to Maui. He went in the morning and found the *kuhina-nui* at her toilet. A maid was brushing her hair before a large mirror. He was welcomed warmly, Kaʻahumanu saying that her "heart had known nothing but joy since the arrival of the ʻVincennes.'" The two old friends engaged in a lively conversation before Stewart mentioned the purpose of his call. Kaʻahumanu immediately offered her pilot boat, a fast schooner, for as long as he wished. The morning of October 19 was settled upon as the day of the departure.[7]

During their first days in Honolulu—indeed throughout their stay—Captain Finch, Charles Stewart, and the officers of the *Vincennes* were widely entertained at parties. At a dinner given by an American, Charles Stewart heard talk which distressed him profoundly. The conversation at table had turned to the character of the young king and the future of his reign. Captain Finch asked if the chiefs had yet decided upon a consort. The American host replied that Nāhiʻenaʻena and Kauikeaouli were deeply attached to each other, that they and many of the chiefs hoped for a marriage between them. This would be in accordance with ancient Hawaiian tradition. The missionaries, however, had taken steps to prevent the union. The American concluded his comments with the statement that a marriage might just as well have taken place, for everyone knew that the king and his sister already lived together "in a state of licentiousness and incest."[8]

"With surprise bordering on indignation," Stewart dropped his knife and fork. Did the host, he asked, actually believe that the royal brother and sister were committing incest? "Most assuredly," the American answered. "Nothing is more notorious—everybody knows it!" To his journal Stewart confided: "Courtesy to me as a guest, and a regard for my feelings, in view of my relation to the princess, and the strong sympathy which I might be known still to feel in all that affects my former associates, should have deterred Mr. — ... from such unqualified defamation, whether unfounded or not. ... These gentlemen were perfectly aware of the attitude in which I stand to the princess.'' Venting his anger in his journal, Stewart recapitulates the history of his relation to Nāhiʻenaʻena—how he had known the girl from her eighth year, how her mother Keōpūolani had committed the child to the ''special guardianship and watchful care of the Rev. Mr. Richards, my colleague, and myself,'' how Nāhiʻenaʻena had been a member of the church in full standing for three years.[9]

Not wanting to believe, he was nonetheless worried. During the next day or two he asked other officers of the *Vincennes* if they had heard such talk. In Honolulu, they said, it was common gossip. Stewart, however, steadfastly refused to believe it until he had made his own investigation.[10]

On October 19, as planned, he sailed in Kaʻahumanu's pilot boat to Maui; there he rejoined his old friends and associates, the Richardses. And there he saw the princess, for the first time in four years. Nāhiʻenaʻena had changed greatly in appearance. She had been a ''slender and delicate child of ten'' when he left Maui. In his imagination she had been transformed into a fairy-tale princess, a child with special distinction, graceful in manner, refined in mind, a girl elevated above others by the royal blood in her veins. Nāhiʻenaʻena was now fourteen. Stewart wrote: ''She is a tall and full grown woman with a form *en bon point*. The rapidity of her growth has been such, that she seems scarce accustomed, her self, to the change in her size; and has lost as much in the gracefulness ... as she has in the elegance of her figure.'' He saw, however, something of the other princess: she retained ''the uncommon brilliance and life of her eye,'' and ''the intelligence, amiability and playfulness of her expression.''[11]

Stewart was not to see much of this playfulness of expression while he was in Lahaina. He brought the unhappy gossip of Honolulu, and he queried Richards about it at the first opportunity. Richards, as pastor of the princess' church, went immediately to Hoapili. Hoapili realized the seriousness of the charge; a council of chiefs must be called. He informed Nāhi-'ena'ena of the report of slander. The girl burst into tears and did not leave her stepfather's house that night. She could not free herself from depression: perhaps for the first time she felt, even though she might not have totally understood, the shame, the fear, of public attack. She did not eat or sleep; she wandered about, distraught, often close to weeping. The people of Lahaina noticed her unusual behavior; one of them was finally bold enough to ask Mrs. Richards about it.[12]

Stewart writes that Mrs. Richards asked the princess about her tears and moodiness. Nāhi'ena'ena answered: ''It is thoughts of Mrs. Stewart. It is sorrow, it is pain, to think how coldly I loved her when here, and how little I, then, regarded her instructions and her advice.'' It seems revealing that she centered her reply on Mrs. Stewart. The remembrance of the missionary wife from whom both she and her mother had taken the baptismal name, Harriet, the return of Stewart himself, bringing back memories and feelings — a recall of the simplicity of the old life — had shaken her. She knew, perhaps for the first time, regret for the loss of childhood and its serenity.[13]

Stewart, probing for the truth, asked his princess if any of the chiefs had suggested a marriage between her and Kauike-aouli. She told the story of the drunken Boki. She also told of another incident, one revealing the mischief perpetrated by unscrupulous Westerners. An Englishman and an American had urged her to marry the king, she said. They claimed that in Europe such unions were frequent — that quite recently, in fact, a British king had married his sister. The American consul, however, had contradicted them; he said that in a Christian country such a marriage was unheard of. Stewart, satisfied with her replies, which corresponded to his deepest wishes and with the evidence of her sorrow, confided to his journal that he had "ascertained, to my perfect satisfaction, that the crimination was as false in fact, as it was heinous in its nature."[14]

When Stewart returned to Honolulu, Nāhiʻenaʻena, Hoapili, and the other "windward chiefs" accompanied him; the council of chiefs was to gather in the capitol. On the morning of his arrival from Lahaina, he called on Kaʻahumanu "to exchange with her an aloha" and also to thank her for the use of the pilot boat. This time he found her dejected, sitting apart from the members of her household, who were at breakfast. She ate nothing. He asked about her melancholy. "There is no sweetness to the food," she said. Her heart was broken because of "the wickedness of the foreigners and the falsehood of their words." The *kuhina-nui* had heard the talk about Nāhiʻenaʻena that very morning.[15]

The council of chiefs centered its deliberations on the injustices of Westerners to Hawaiians. They composed a letter to Captain Finch asking his help in securing amends for the treatment of local residents by foreigners. Over a period of years, Americans and British had behaved with arrogance and frequent cruelty toward Hawaiian people. The situation had come to a climax in a brutal act, one that became symbolic of the many injustices Hawaiians had suffered from people who were alien to their kingdom. The incident commenced in a simple, pastoral way. A cow belonging to the British consul had repeatedly strayed from his "plantation" and browsed on the land of a Hawaiian. Exasperated after a long effort to have the consul confine his animal, the Hawaiian killed the cow. In retaliation the British and American consuls tied the islander behind their horses and dragged him for two miles. Before the arrival of the *Vincennes*, a letter had been composed by the chiefs protesting this wrong, but nothing had come of it. They now addressed Captain Finch in the hope the American naval officer could assist. They included in the same letter the issue of Nāhiʻenaʻena and wrote of "the false and lying report . . . concerning the Princess Nahienaena, that she is a lewd and incestuous woman." They claimed that their hearts were broken by such scandal. The letter was signed not only by the king, Kaʻahumanu, and other important chiefs, but also by Nāhiʻenaʻena.[16]

When Stewart recorded the letter in his journal, he left out the words, "lewd and incestuous," which appear in the official document. He could not bring himself to put down such strong language about his princess. His writings, however, show that he suffered from doubt. He could not present himself, he said, "in pledge for the continued integrity, and future fair fame" of Harriet. He recognized that she lived in circumstances that continually threatened her "brightness and spirituality of Christian character."[17]

Stewart consoled himself—tried to allay his doubt and worry—by writing of the many incidents of the princess' gracious behavior and describing her elegant dress during the round of festivities during the visit of the *Vincennes*. Captain Finch first met Nāhiʻenaʻena on the occasion of his formal call upon the chiefs from Maui and Hawaiʻi. She wore a fashionable gown of straw-colored satin, and her hair was arranged with combs. Her manners were dignified, Stewart records, and

she expressed herself with animation. She made a good impression on the captain "as an intelligent and fine young woman." The "father" of the royal "daughter" clung tenacious-
ly to his dream of her refinement and distinction. When she
visited aboard the *Vincennes*, she wore purple silk velvet; at
King Kauikeaouli's dinner party she was gowned in white satin embroidered in gold. For a picnic in Nuʻuanu Valley, she
was dramatic in a black dress with a mantle of scarlet satin;
her hat was of white silk decorated with flowers. Even her
horse matched the costume—he was glossy black. She was, as
he had said in Lahaina, a "full grown woman."[18]

In his book *Visit to the South Seas*, he devoted a chapter to
the picnic in the valley. On a bright morning when the trade
winds were fresh, the cavalcade of guests and Hawaiian chiefs
set out from the palace yard. Their final destination was the
country home of Boki and Liliha; but first, the guests would be
taken to see the famous *pali*, cliff, which had figured prominently in King Kamehameha's battle for the island of Oʻahu.
The party left Honolulu and rode across the streams and
through the woods of Nuʻuanu, following the course of a carriage road under construction. They went first to the cliff.
There the young king, "in a handsome riding suit and mounted on a noble animal," told the story of the battle and of his
father's prowess as a warrior. At his side, seated on her black
horse, was his sister in black gown and red mantle. Stewart's
romantic imagination was roused by the spectacle; he could
see in his mind's eye the fighting, more than three decades
earlier, of "thousands of a savage race in all the fury of a
deadly conflict . . . amidst the brandishment and hurling of
spears and war club." And he gazed proudly upon Nāhiʻena-
ʻena and Kauikeaouli: "Would you believe the civilized

brother and sister . . . to be the son and the daughter of the most fearful of the leaders of the savage horde?"[19]

After hearing about the exploits of Kamehameha I and gazing on the sweep of the windward side of the island, the party went to Boki's country home. Inside the simple cottage, a picnic luncheon was served for the king, the princess, Ka'ahumanu, and the honored guests from the *Vincennes*. Though they sat on fine mats on the ground, the china and glassware were of the most elegant, as if set on a rosewood table. The meal was sumptuous—baked fish, roast pig, chicken, potatoes, taro; madeira, muscadine, and claret wine. Liliha concluded the meal in her own fashion—with a gentle mockery of the Westerners. A servant set before her a package wrapped in cresses and green leaves, dripping with cool water. "While her eye brightened more and more with pleasantry," she untied the package and "suddenly scattered the contents—a quantity of live shrimp, as pure and transparent as could be, and as sprightly as crickets—over the cresses." Then laughing, she picked up a handful and popped them into her mouth. The ever-courteous Captain Finch, though hardly accustomed to such a diet, took a handful too. One of them, at least, found its way into his mouth.[20]

The mission took the occasion of the visit of the *Vincennes* to hold an examination of the students of the schools it had established throughout O'ahu. The chiefs took advantage of this public examination to arrange a pageant of their own to display for the American officers the ancient beauty and traditional dignity of Hawai'i. The events took place in Kawaiaha'o Church. While two-thirds of the building was reserved for the schools, one-third was set apart for the chiefesses. "With all the ancient paraphernalia of chieftainship, they [were] borne in procession from their respective residences to the chapel." In the church, they were grouped formally according to rank.[21]

The princess was the center of the tableau. She sat on a high platform which had been draped in many thicknesses of *kapa*, the ends hanging in graceful folds to the floor. Behind her, young chiefs dressed in yellow and scarlet feather cloaks held thirty-foot multicolored *kāhili*. Nāhiʻenaʻena was clad, almost symbolically, in dual fashion. She wore a loose gown of black satin with high neck and long sleeves to preserve her Christian modesty. Over it was spread the magnificent yellow feather skirt lined in red satin which she had worn at Liholiho's funeral, and on her shoulders was a yellow feather cloak with designs in red and black. She had leis of feathers around her neck and on her hair. Near her on smaller and lower platforms sat the other distinguished chiefesses, each with *kāhili* bearers. Stewart comments that the whole formed a "semicircle of aboriginal splendor." Curiously enough, Kaʻahumanu, dressed in European style, stood in the background holding a *kāhili*, "as in the train of the princess." Stewart does not mention the king in the pageant at the church.[22]

Captain Finch and the officers were seated thirty feet away from the chiefesses. When the captain recognized Nāhiʻenaʻena, he rose and bowed. She acknowledged his courtesy by removing the feather cape and sending it to him by a young chief. The captain placed the cloak about his shoulders and wore it while he watched the students of the mission display their skills in reading, writing, arithmetic.[23]

Captain Finch and Stewart had heard that at the conclusion of the ceremony the chiefesses would leave in procession; thus they hurried from the church to the upper verandah of the prime minister's house, where they had a fine view of the whole street. The parade was led by two children of high rank seated on a couch of state. Unlike Nāhiʻenaʻena and Kauikea-ouli at the same age, these young chiefs were unused to being carried in traditional fashion and surrounded by tall *kāhili*; they screamed so mightily that their attendants had to take them into their arms. The dowager queens followed the children. After them, escorted by the royal guards, walked the king and his suite. The climax of the procession was the appearance of Nāhiʻenaʻena, borne on her large platform. Guards had to clear passage for the royal equipage through the gaily dressed throngs of people. Stewart was eloquent.

> . . . for she who was thus borne aloft, surrounded by all the glory of her rank and the gaze of ten thousand eyes, was the joy of the people and the delight of the whole nation. And while I gazed in admiration on the animated and youthful favorite passing triumphantly along, beneath a canopy of magnificent kahiles nodding with grace and stateliness in the breeze—I thought, and remarked, that the pageant, though destitute of gilding of equipage and caparison of horse found in other countries, equalled, if it did not surpass, in its effect upon the eye and upon the heart, the most gorgeous and princely train I ever witnessed.[24]

In November when the *Vincennes* was ready to depart, Captain Finch invited Nāhiʻenaʻena and the windward chiefs to take passage back to their respective islands. The first port of call was Lahaina, where the princess disembarked. There, in his old home, Stewart took leave of her. She gave him a letter for Mrs. Stewart; it was written at a time when she could see clearly her dilemma—that whatever she did was a violation or a trespass or a sin in one or the other of the two worlds in which she lived. The letter begins, "Where art thou, my greatly beloved mother, Mrs. Stewart?" She speaks of her regret that they could no longer meet and their "eyes no more fall upon each other." She expresses affection for the Stewart children. Then she attempts to reveal to her "mother" the state of her mind. Though she lives among Christians and performs the acts of Christian worship, she writes, her heart is not steadfast; it wavers. She prays daily to God that he will "establish his kingdom" in her heart. At the end of her letter, she brings us close to her feelings, as she writes lucidly and intimately. Though frequently her mind is tempted by the many passing trifles, her soul desires to practice the way of piety. She hopes ardently to reach a state of grace. She admits that not a single day "passes without sin. One day my thoughts are fixed on God; another day I am ensnared: and thus it is continually." Significantly, she signs the letter, "Harieta Keopuolani."[25]

"Thus it is continually." Nāhiʻenaʻena, in a moment of revelation, recognized that she was "ensnared." The word "ensnared" speaks eloquently. It reveals a moment of insight, almost a prophesy of her own doom.

12

"The Brink of Destruction"

After the pomp of Honolulu—after what amounted to a kind of apotheosis, as Nāhiʻenaʻena basked in the affection and approval of both Charles Stewart and her own people—Lahaina now seemed a place of eternal boredom. The princess complained that the village was "dirty." She said she wanted to move to Wailuku and ordered workers to build a road over the mountains to this cooler, rainier spot. The dirtiness was dust, certainly; Lahaina was a dry spot in spite of the luxuriance of taro and banana patches. But the dirtiness had further dimensions. Lorrin Andrews gazed upon her with disapproving and critical eye; William Richards hovered anxiously. The Christianized Hawaiians frowned at some of the habits she had brought from Honolulu—card playing, wine drinking, listening to music.

Her boredom and restrained anger burst into intermittent displays of defiance and irrationality. She began to interrupt Sabbath meetings. It delighted her to arrive late, just before the conclusion of the services. She entered the church with her retinue, striding noisily up the aisle in search of a seat. Andrews wrote to Chamberlain that her trip to Honolulu had been a "great disadvantage."[1]

Nāhiʻenaʻena's outbursts reflect not only her own inner struggle but the struggle within the nation as well. The early 1830s were often alarming years. The Hawaiians had had enough of mission restraint, and they erupted anew into lawless ways. Drunkenness, theft, murder, adultery greatly increased. The king offered no example to his people. He traveled restlessly with the Hulumanu and was often drunk; he gambled, held large entertainments of dancing and singing, and enjoyed a series of mistresses. He disregarded the counsel of both Kaʻahumanu and the missionaries. Because of his rank, there were occasions when even those highly placed dared not interfere.

For nearly a year, Nāhiʻenaʻena once again all but vanishes from the letters and records kept by the missionaries. We can only deduce from later accounts that she spent many despairing hours of confusion, that she enjoyed occasional happy periods with her brother whenever she was summoned to Honolulu, and again days when she moodily withdrew into her Lahaina household, drinking wine, playing cards, listening to the ancient chants. Suddenly, in October 1830, she made a dramatic, desperate move. She went to William Richards and asked if she might live in his house. What compelled her to do this? Was it fear? Was it desire for attention? Often she appeared to believe in Christian precepts and to understand something about sin. She may have had visions of hellfire. Or perhaps there was a deeper unconscious fear. She was lost. She was neither princess nor Christian woman in the turbulent world which had grown up around her. Exalted, she was nevertheless living on the periphery of Hawaiian affairs.

In his letter to Chamberlain, Richards describes the young woman's impulsive feelings. "You will be surprised to learn that the princess has taken up her abode with us. She has fitted up one of our chambers in which she lodges and takes about half of her meals at our table." His household, he writes, was thrown into "trouble and confusion," but he welcomed this "lamb of my charge." He had observed her for the past year, his tears had often flowed and his spirits had sunk as he watched her "near the brink of destruction." For her to make such a move — to ask to live in the simple missionary home, probably with only an attendant or two — suggests that Nāhiʻenaʻena herself felt near the "brink of destruction."

Richards writes that he was willing to devote his life to Nāhiʻenaʻena's welfare if he could become the means through which she might be transformed into an "adornment" of her royal position. He was convinced that in guiding her firmly into the ways of a Christian gentlewoman, he could save at least a part of a whole generation of people. He never forgot the political and dynastic implications of her person. "For while she lives like a Christian we have a powerful hold on the king but should she fall to human appearance she carries her brother and consequently the nation with her." Yet he was not optimistic about Nāhiʻenaʻena's future. She appeared for the moment to be happy in his household. "Yet we do not hope for much more than to keep her from those former temptations which had proved so nearly fatal." As might be expected, she did not remain long in Richards' home.[2]

Nor did she remain the "lamb of his charge." A year after her sudden move into the Richards home, the princess was reported to be drinking again. She publicly acknowledged her guilt and confessed that her "crime" had been committed on September 18, 1831. In November the church suspended Nāhiʻenaʻena from communion, and she was asked to sit apart from the congregation. She was reinstated in December after a church resolution found "that she had given evidence of sincerity." For a while Richards remained in some control. Early in 1832 he wrote Chamberlain that she continued to show good behavior—better than during the past two or three years. She had become disgusted with her brother because of his dissolute ways and had written him not to come down for the dedication of the new church at Lahaina. Richards writes: "I <u>hope</u> [she] feels something as she ought." He used portentous words: "hope" which he underlined, and "ought" which expresses the essence of the Puritan position. Nāhiʻenaʻena, as sacred chiefess, never understood "oughtness" in the Christian sense.[3]

Kaʻahumanu was ill. In the hope of finding better health, she decided to move permanently from Honolulu to her quiet cottage in the cool air of Mānoa Valley. Her servants carried her tenderly and gently on a litter, protected from the sun by a shade. At the fresh springs of Punahou, the party paused for rest; then it journeyed the remaining three miles up the valley to the cottage. Hiram Bingham rises to one of his rhetorical flourishes as he describes the significance of her move. She went "among the mountains, as one retiring from the cares of office, the guardianship of the State, the agitations of Honolulu, the bustle of the world, and the sorrows of a life of almost three-score years, five-sixths of which had been spent in heathenism." In her cottage, Kaʻahumanu lay on a fragrant bed of sweet-scented *maile* and ginger leaves over which had been spread a velvet cover. The chiefs and the missionaries gathered around her. Outside in the woods and fields the common-ers had built temporary dwellings of branches in which they lived, paying a last tribute of sorrow.

Nāhiʻenaʻena was summoned from Lahaina to watch with the others over the old queen. She joined her brother Kauike-aouli and her half-sister Kīnaʻu at the bedside. Kaʻahumanu had close to her the three children of her husband Kameha-meha—the three in whose hands lay the destiny of the king-dom. Hiram Bingham writes that during the *kuhina-nui*'s ill-ness the printing of the translation of the New Testament was completed. The missionaries quickly had a copy bound in red morocco and engraved in gold with Kaʻahumanu's name. He presented it to her; she "took the sacred prize in her hands" and leafed through the pages, then carefully wrapped it in a handkerchief and placed it on her bosom. "*Maikai,*" good, she said. Thus the venerable and once powerful old woman spent her last hours with the great chiefs of her race and the *palapala* of her new religion. She died just before dawn on June 5, 1832.[4] The nation had lost the last of the rulers who had lived and flourished in the ancient tradition. As was cus-tomary, a chant was composed for her death:

> Floating on the dizzy way to the unknown land;
> Here a moment ago, now gone. . . .
>
> Treading as a chief on her way,
> On the ebb tide slipping and diving,
> The chiefess has fallen asleep and left,
> Flying away at the time of dawn.[5]

On July 5 the chiefs gathered in council to proclaim Kīnaʻu, daughter of Kamehameha, successor to Kaʻahumanu. Kauike-aouli gave her the title Kaʻahumanu II. Addressing the people, he again proclaimed that the laws of the land were to be based on the laws of God. He decreed that a man's land could not be taken from him unless he was guilty of a breach of the law of God. He commanded that the joint words of Kīnaʻu and himself should be obeyed.[6]

On that same day Nāhiʻenaʻena returned to Lahaina.

With the death of the great _kuhina-nui_ and the approach of Kauikeaouli's majority, the turbulence in the nation increased. Beneath the external events and their political consequences a deeper cultural force was emerging. The people had returned to the hula and the old music, to Hawaiian games and customs. The historian Kuykendall suggests that this marked a revival of Hawaiian tradition; it constituted a groping effort to restore and renew an ancient identity which had eroded since the overthrow of the _kapu_ and during the growing dominance of the mission—an identity which was in danger of disappearing. Kuykendall labels this period with its political, cultural, and economic difficulties "the troubled thirties."

Kauikeaouli, early in 1833, abandoned all restraint. He excluded from his presence the chiefs who tried to control him; he remained deaf to the missionaries. He charted his own way: a continual round of noisy parties, heavy drinking, horse racing and gambling, women. He started the revival of ancient forms of the hula and the old sports, such as the Hawaiian versions of bowling and dart throwing. He entertained himself in exaggerated and ludicrous fashion: when his pet baboon died, he had the animal buried in a coffin with a mock Christian ceremony. On another occasion he sent a crier through the streets to summon all prostitutes to pay court to his mistress and bring tribute to her. In March his antics came to a climax.

He announced the repeal of all laws in the kingdom except those against theft and murder.[7]

In part, his behavior may be attributed to conflict with Kīnaʻu. She had refused to allow him to purchase a brig that he very much wanted. He was in a rage with her—a king's rage—and rumors circulated through the capitol that he might replace Kīnaʻu with the more capricious Liliha. His continued defiance culminated on March 14, 1833. He sent a crier through the capital summoning the people to his residence on the next day; at that time he would deliver a *manaʻo*, a statement of his thought. To Kīnaʻu's residence he sent two officers of the government in formal dress; one was Kaomi, a leader of the Hulumanu. They presented the *kuhina-nui* with a communication which stated the king's intent: He would take for himself all lands conquered by Kamehameha, his father, but would grant to others lands taken by their fathers in conquest. He would assume control over life and death, right and wrong. He would establish in his own name the laws for the nation.

On the following day, the chiefs gathered in formal fashion while the commoners crowded the open space that had been designated. When Kīnaʻu arrived, the king ordered that a way be cleared for her. As they met, he pressed his nose to hers in the Hawaiian fashion of greeting. She took her assigned seat on the ground. The king then leaned down and whispered to her, inviting her to make a statement. But she deferred to him. He then rose and announced to the people the substance of his message to Kīnaʻu. He added that she was to be the *noho hale* for him and the *imi hale* for the other chiefs. He was alluding to an earlier saying that Kamehameha had established the dynasty (*imi hale*) and Liholiho had occupied it (*noho hale*). Thus, contrary to the expectations of some, he appointed nei-

129

ther Liliha nor the unscrupulous Kaomi as his premier. Kīnaʻu who had some of the strength and wisdom of Kaʻahumanu remained the *kuhina-nui*. When asked after the ceremony why he had selected his sister, the king said: "Very strong is the kingdom of God."[8]

While Kauikeaouli, with all the vigor, restlessness, and rebelliousness of a young chief, led his own wayward life and took action to end the regency, Nāhiʻenaʻena remained in the quiet of Lahaina. Early in 1833 there was brief talk of a marriage for her. Missionaries and chiefs alike, in view of the recurring gossip about her and the king, wanted to have her safely married to a ranking chief. The chiefs chose a young man whose father was the first-born son of Kamehameha I. Richards calls him a "villain," but the reason for this is not given, and there is no further statement about him save a notice of his death a year later.[9]

Occasionally Nāhiʻenaʻena expressed worry about the actions of her brother. She knew that Hoapili was frequently summoned to Honolulu because of the king's behavior. And she made a small gesture of her own. She sent a letter by the youngest of Liholiho's widows, a chiefess who regularly resided in Lahaina. The letter urged the king to give up his drunkenness and curb his extravagant antics. Kauikeaouli, when he received it, played one of his childish pranks. He offered the chiefess a glass of "spirits" and invited her to drink with him. She refused. He insisted. He was, after all, the king, and she, though under mission guidance, could not refuse a few sips. Her "fall from grace" was reported in Lahaina. After her return, she was watched over with great concern.[10]

When Hoapili brought to Lahaina the news of Kauikeaouli's defiance of Kīnaʻu, Nāhiʻenaʻena was distressed. She

recognized that a break with the premier would have grave re-
percussions throughout the nation. She brooded for some time
and spent sleepless nights. Richards records that he talked
and prayed with her an entire afternoon, seeking to bring her
calm.[11]

Though in March, Kauikeaouli had reaffirmed Kīna'u as
kuhina-nui, his differences with her did not end. They ex-
ploded again early in June. Kīna'u's husband, Kekuana'o'a,
was commander of the king's guards and thus had charge of
the weapons of the nation. Without warning, the king ordered
Kīna'u to give up the guns and her husband's commission.
She went immediately to confer with Kauikeaouli. He explained that it was not the guns he wanted but the resignation
of Kekuana'o'a, because he wished to give the commission to
a half-caste friend. She spoke bluntly to the king, so bluntly
that he finally told her to leave. Before she left, she warned
that she would call in all firearms and take charge of them
herself until Hoapili and the princess could come from Maui
for a council. Then the appropriate person could be selected
to command the guard and take charge of the arms. The chiefs
in council would also clarify the prerogatives of the king.[12]

The chiefs assembled in Honolulu. But the king boycotted
their meeting and amused himself in his usual fashion with the
Hulumanu. After a month of conferences the chiefs decided
that the only solution was to get Kauikeaouli, willing or unwilling, to go to Lahaina. Levi Chamberlain urged the chiefs to
use persuasion, not force. He pointed out that the reactions of
foreigners to the council's decision might be dangerous, for
they had considerable economic and political power in the
kingdom. Many foreigners took the king's side simply because
they enjoyed his parties and his buffoonery. The chiefs agreed
with Chamberlain and decided to use Nāhi'ena'ena as instru-

ment of persuasion. There is no record of what was said between brother and sister, but the king apparently promised
that he would go.

On the evening of the sailing, the princess called for her
brother at his residence. The two walked hand in hand down to
the quay—the princess, according to Kamakau, with an arm
around her brother's neck. When they passed the house of a
Mr. French, an American, the king asked to be excused. He
went inside, where a group of foreigners had gathered for the
purpose of detaining him. Kauikeaouli did not return that
night to Nāhi'ena'ena. "He had vanished leaving his sister
weeping and wailing for her brother." Accompanied by two
high chiefs, she sailed for Maui without him.[13]

13

Brother and Sister

Around 1827 a man for whom records are indistinct or confusing entered Nāhiʻenaʻena's life. According to the newspaper account of his death he was born in Dartmouth, Massachusetts, and came of a "well-known and respectably connected family." He was a ship's captain; but he seems not always to have been the best of navigators. Attempting one dark night to sail between east and west Maui, he ran his ship aground near Kahului. News of the wreck reached the princess, and she sent help to him and his sailors. She became so attached to Abe Russell that, in the fashion of Hawaiian chiefs, she adopted him as her "son." After the "adoption," Russell began to spend a good deal of time in Lahaina, probably as a member of the princess' household, though intermittently he continued his career at sea. In a letter to the king from Lahaina dated August 2, 1831, he speaks of having had a pleasant passage, presumably from Honolulu; then he adds that the princess sends her best regards. The letter has many misspelled words and the elliptical syntax of one unused to writing; its tone is familiar.[1]

No one has paid much attention to the sparse details of what may have been a romance between a rough Yankee and a Polynesian princess. We know enough of Nāhiʻenaʻena's temperament to realize that Abe Russell could have been her lover; we know enough about the responses of American seamen to speculate that Russell would hardly have rejected a person of such exalted rank. The meager recorded facts, however, do not permit anything but the wildest kind of guessing. What we do know is that Abe Russell accepted the patronage of the princess. On her deathbed, she charged Kauikeaouli and the high chiefs with the care of her "son." Russell thus became a pensioner of the royal family until his death in 1875. He continued his career at sea until he managed another wreck, that of the bark *Drymo* at Lahaina in 1845. The royal accounts show that during the years 1867 to 1868, in the reign of Kamehameha V, sums of $500 or more were given once a month to Russell. This was a considerable sum at the time. His obituary in the *Pacific Commercial Advertiser* states that he lived in a neat cottage on the palace grounds; that the king and queen not only attended his funeral services but that the royal coach followed immediately after the hearse on the way to Nuʻuanu Cemetery.[2]

Another dimension of the princess' attachment to Abe Russell is suggested in a letter written in 1901 by Sereno Bishop, son of Artemas Bishop of the second company of missionaries. He tells of a story he heard some twenty years after Nāhiʻenaʻena's death. Once, when Russell was about to embark on a whaleship from Lahaina, Nāhiʻenaʻena tried to prevent his departure. Bishop, reporting from hearsay alone, writes of her "wild and insane public clinging" to the man. He concludes the account with a terse statement that Abe remained with the princess and was taken care of for life.[3]

The wild clinging to a seaman on the beach at Lahaina; the sorrowful wailing on the Honolulu quay after Kauikeaouli entered the doorway of Mr. French's house: these suggest that Nāhiʻenaʻena no longer controlled the province of her life. The dual self—its conflicts and dilemmas—which began at that unrecorded moment when Keōpūolani first offered her daughter to Richards as a pupil in reading and writing, had eroded the force of her will; the duality had muddled her roles—what she was to the kingdom and what she was within herself. She had become the victim, ironically, of her mother's hopes and of Richards' and Stewart's training. She was also victim of her own strong passions.

In Lahaina, Lorrin Andrews wrote ominously that she took "every thief and whoremonger into her train." This was missionary rhetoric. Who were the thieves and whoremongers? Perhaps chiefs and chiefesses, companions, attendants, who enjoyed with her some of the mission-forbidden pleasures, people who did not press her with torrents of pious words or threats of damnation. They probably played cards in her household, drank wine, danced, listened to the old music, to the chants which compared the princess to the forces of nature—to red flowers, flames of lava, springs of fresh water, to the sun—and exalted her as a god. They certainly brought comfort to a lost and confused young woman, a royal princess who was virtually in exile.[4]

Nāhiʻenaʻena revealed in December 1833, almost pathetically, something of the extent of her suffering because of this exile. Hoapili, who had been spending considerable time in

Honolulu on the king's account, returned home to Lahaina for a short visit. When he was ready to go back to Honolulu, Nāhi-ʻenaʻena begged him to take her with him. Still feeling herself under mission control, however, she asked William Richards for his consent. Richards hesitated. Oʻahu, he knew only too well, spelled disaster. Once again she would be in the court circle, sharing its flamboyant activities. And most distressing of all, she would be close to Kauikeaouli. Lahaina, however, was no longer a secure haven for her. With Hoapili and his wife away most of the time, no chief remained in the village who had either the authority or the persuasiveness to cope with her moods and waywardness. Though in many respects Richards was the person closest to the princess' inner feelings, he reluctantly admitted that his influence with the girl had diminished. He understood clearly the reasons. In the last three years or so he had often opposed her wishes, and it had been difficult to make her either feel or understand the principles on which his challenge was based. Frequently his efforts to keep her in the Christian path served to drive her further toward dissipation. (Lorrin Andrews, who shared the mission post with Richards, was much sharper in his judgment. He wrote that Nāhiʻenaʻena hung "like a millstone about all that is good here.") Richards, accordingly, weighed the advantages and disadvantages for the princess of a visit to Honolulu. He finally consented to her going.

Hoapili decided not to leave Lahaina until after the first Sunday in January 1834. It was an important day for the mission, the celebration of communion. This delay gave William Richards a short period of grace in which to appeal to whatever Christian feeling and conviction he had implanted in Nāhiʻenaʻena. His sense of urgency was great, and heightened by the realization that he might never again have a chance to save his princess. The depth of devotion to his religious belief and conscience, and to Nāhiʻenaʻena herself, is revealed in his letters at the time. He was making, he felt, a last-ditch stand. He talked long hours with Nāhiʻenaʻena, he prayed with her, he used all the powers of his affection, his persuasion and logic. He aroused her shame, and she wept; she saw clearly and lamented openly her many failings as a Christian. Richards watched the flow of tears and dared to hope that it was evidence of genuine Christian feeling. He was, however, filled with foreboding.

On the evening before embarkation for Honolulu, Hoapili sent for Richards. He went to the chief's house and found the princess with her guardian; they were talking of her marriage, and they wanted her teacher to share in the deliberation. Nāhiʻenaʻena expressed disapproval of Keola, the man the chiefs had earlier selected for her and the one whom the missionary had called a "villain." She preferred Leleiōhoku, a young man of distinguished ancestry whose guardian was Kuakini, governor of the island of Hawaiʻi. In the course of the evening, Hoapili suggested that Nāhiʻenaʻena's visit to Oʻahu be a short one; after her return, she could send a ship to bring Leleiōhoku and Kuakini to Maui and the marriage could be planned in more complete detail. In the event that Kuakini wanted the ceremony to take place on Hawaiʻi, she could travel there. Nāhiʻenaʻena said that if the marriage were celebrated on Hawaiʻi, she wanted Richards to accompany her. The missionary quickly promised to escort the "lamb" who had been placed in his charge. Her request, he hoped, was a sign of Christian piety.

The clergyman went to the beach the following day to bid farewell to Nāhiʻenaʻena. She took him by the hand; her mood was gentle and affectionate. She reminded him of his promise the evening before; and she reassured him that her visit to Oʻahu would not be long.[5]

The ship that carried Nāhiʻenaʻena to Honolulu carried also a letter from Richards to Levi Chamberlain. He expressed anxiety about the effect of the court circle on the well-being of the princess and asked Chamberlain to watch over her and to invite her frequently to his home. Richards knew that it was essential for the girl to be frequently in the company of missionaries so that she might practice the ways of a Christian gentlewoman. Nāhiʻenaʻena, he realized, had often depended on him; because of their long association and affection, she had sought his approval for her actions, and she valued her membership in the church. In Honolulu, she would be far away, and much could happen; she could move, unknown to him, toward the brink of destruction.[6]

Chamberlain hurried to do Richards' bidding. Soon after the princess' arrival he invited her, the king, and the high chiefs to tea. Everyone came but the king. In his usual laconic fashion, Chamberlain gives no details of the affair—simply the bare facts. We may imagine it was a conventional missionary party, with plain food, conversation, and perhaps singing of hymns. Such an occasion could scarcely attract the dissolute Kauikeaouli.[7]

Nāhiʻenaʻena's stay in Honolulu was not short; the weeks stretched into months. The marriage arrangements in which her teacher was to share seemed forgotten. She wrote friendly letters to Richards in January, February, and April; no rumors reached him that gave cause for worry.

In March, Nāhiʻenaʻena commenced a tour, a royal progress, around the island of Oʻahu. Her retinue included Hoapili, a large company of chiefs, and the king. Kauikeaouli planned to travel as far as Ewa with his favorite Kaomi and other Hulumanu. A missionary journeyed with the cavalcade: Dr. Judd, at the "urgent request" of Kīnaʻu, accompanied the princess. The *kuhina-nui*'s anxiety suggests that the important chiefs were troubled. They were in a position to observe the private details of Nāhiʻenaʻena's Honolulu life, and they realized that her feeling for her brother and his for her contained dangers not only for the young sacred chiefs but for the kingdom. Kauikeaouli in his present mood could not be held responsible; he was wholly committed to debauchery.

On the second or third day of the tour, the king began to indulge in his usual excesses. Returning from a swim, he seized women at random and attempted to force them to his will. He may have been drunk at the time—certainly he was consuming large quantities of *ʻawa*, the Hawaiian narcotic drink. Dr. Judd wrote the mission that he was determined to remain close by the princess' side.[8]

After a ten-day stop at Ewa, Nāhiʻenaʻena left her brother and continued her royal journey. She moved at a leisurely pace from village to village; it was a happy freedom she did not often have on Maui, where usually the missionaries were with her, wanting to hurry from school to church to school. At each town the people crowded to honor the princess, Hoapili, and the other chiefs; they presented the gifts of their harvest—vegetables, pigs, chickens, fruits, flowers. They gave parties for her entertainment. Dr. Judd wrote that at many of the stops Hoapili addressed the people, urging them to give up the use of spirituous liquor and advising them to attend school to learn their letters. At some of the villages the princess also spoke, echoing the substance of Hoapili's message. The progress served two purposes, one royal and the other Christian. Like a chiefess of old, indeed, like a princess of any country,

Nāhiʻenaʻena gave the people an opportunity to look upon her and hear her. As a Christian she urged the virtues of the faith.[9]

The tour lasted a month. Nāhiʻenaʻena returned to Honolulu in time to attend the baptism of Kīnaʻu's infant son, born February 9, 1834. She was disappointed that the baby was a boy, for Kīnaʻu had promised the child, if a girl, to the princess to rear. The boy, however, was promised to the king. On April 27 the infant was christened Alexander Liholiho, and in time he would succeed his adoptive father as Kamehameha IV. During the ceremony, Kīnaʻu held the baby for the "application of water"; Kauikeaouli was at her side. Somewhere in the background among the other chiefs stood Kekuanaʻoʻa, the infant's father.[10]

Kauikeaouli's drunkenness and disorderly conduct seemed by now to be chronic. Plagued, it appears, with profound inner discontent, driven by desire and confusion, he moved feverishly about the island of Oʻahu. One of his favorite spots was a retreat at Pearl River, in Puʻuloa. There, far enough from the disapproving eyes of the missionaries and of Kīnaʻu, Hoapili, and other high chiefs, he indulged in the sensuality which served his inner frustrations. His life, if he bothered to reflect, must have seemed rife with contradictions: he had proclaimed himself king, yet he was not king; the power was not his—it was Kīnaʻu's. He did not understand what it meant to be a ruler. The nation had rapidly moved away from old sanctioned patterns toward a new, puzzling society. In the midst of the political and social ferment, an epidemic had swept the island and claimed a great many Hawaiians. Among those who died were two linked closely to the king and his sister: the daughter of Kuakini, who had been selected by the chiefs as royal consort for Kauikeaouli, and Keola, whom the chiefs had chosen as husband for Nāhiʻenaʻena and whom she had rejected. Death once again struck the chiefly ranks, as it had so often done since the coming of the Westerner.[11]

Early in June 1834, Kauikeaouli went to his retreat in Puʻuloa. It was, we may imagine, another of his attempts to escape whatever routine affairs of government he was involved in, the restraints of the mission and the powerful chiefs — perhaps even a reaction to the horrors of death from the epidemic; he needed almost continuously to indulge his desire for excitement, change, and drink. This time he wanted his sister with him, and he sent a ship to Honolulu to bring her to Pearl River. She refused to go. It was said she feared the disapproval of Hoapili. The day after this rebuff, shocking news reached Honolulu. The king had attempted suicide.[12]

The chiefs rushed to him; Dr. Judd, Dr. Rooke, and Mr. Bingham were summoned. The Westerners found the king resting in a small grass house. His bed stood in a dark corner partitioned by a curtain from the rest of the room. Kauikeaouli greeted his visitors courteously. When the doctors asked him about his symptoms, he refused to answer. When they spoke of the state of his soul, he remained silent. Finally, Dr. Judd asked if he wished any medicine, and he made a sign that he did not.[13]

We shall probably never know the precise details; they are muffled in confusing, contradictory accounts. Most reports agree that the king attempted to slash his throat and drown himself; he was rescued from the water by one of his retainers. Honolulu was filled with speculation and gossip: some claimed that Kauikeaouli was depressed over the deaths of Kuakini's daughter and Keola; others agreed with the missionaries that he had acted in a fit of drunkenness. Levi Chamberlain wrote that Dr. Judd had questioned the Hawaiians at Puʻuloa and "satisfied himself that the king had been at least for a time in a state of mental derangement. The cause was probably the excessive use of strong drink. This perhaps in connexion with other things." A modern historian has speculated that he was despondent over Nāhiʻenaʻena's refusal to come to him—that he had wanted to marry her. The gossipy merchant Stephen Reynolds sums up the speculations in his journal: "All guessed, none knew."[14]

The king's injuries were not serious, and a week later he was back in Honolulu.

Nāhiʻenaʻena's refusal to go to Puʻuloa and the king's attempted suicide were, if not prophetic, at least symptomatic of the step which the brother and sister must inevitably take. The anguish of thwarted love, the continued threat of death: these two are often the companions of men caught in the drive of passion. They are usually present when one culture impinges upon another, creating confusion, a clash of wills, and a desire for old harmonies. With Kauikeaouli and Nāhiʻenaʻena, the mission had failed. The great chiefs, many of them Christians, were compelled to yield to a long-nurtured royal desire, firmly grounded in the traditions of the nation.

On a night in late July in the house of the high chief Paki, Kauikeaouli and Nāhiʻenaʻena married. They married in the ancient way of chiefs: the king slept with his sister in the presence of their guardians Hoapili and his wife, of a half-sister who had been the youngest wife of Liholiho, and others of rank. Afterwards, the royal couple wrote a letter to Kīnaʻu informing her of their marriage. And the king sent a crier through the streets to proclaim the royal event.

Honolulu—the whole kingdom—rocked with the news. In an effort to protect their union, the royal bride and groom shut themselves away from all who clamored at their doorway. To keep privacy, the king was forced to have his house patrolled by the armed guard. The Christian chiefs and the missionaries persisted in trying to reach the royal pair to argue and plead with them, to dissuade them from their marriage. The king threatened to retire to remote Wai'anae, at the far end of the island. For a while the young couple clung to what they had: the power of their love, the fantasy that love would prevail, the hope they could escape their tormentors. He was king; she was the only woman of sufficient rank to be his wife. They were bound to each other by shared childhood and by tradition. Their love grew in spite of the Western attitudes toward incest, in spite of their enforced separation when missionaries and chiefs kept Nāhi'ena'ena exiled in Lahaina, in spite of their love affairs with other persons. An inevitable love and a deep one, it had endured long; unfortunately it carried seeds of tragedy and death.[15]

It was almost dawn in Lahaina. John I'ī, a distinguished attendant of the king, a Christian, knocked on William Richards' door. He announced the news of the royal incestuous marriage. Richards, as deeply shaken as he had ever been, made a dramatic gesture. It sprang, probably, from the knowledge of his own successes and failures in guiding the royal family, and from the memory of his beloved patroness. He went to the tomb of Keōpūolani; there he wrote Nāhi'ena'ena a long letter. He reminded her of her mother's last days, of her hopes for her daughter, of her dying charges. Then he selected a man of importance and rank to carry the missive to Honolulu, one who would be certain to gain access to the princess.

The messenger found Nāhi'ena'ena among a large company of guests and attendants; they were enjoying recitations and chants of ancient legends. When she learned that a courier had come from Richards, she dismissed all but two or three persons. The courier entered and presented the letter. She broke the seal and read a few lines, perhaps those which told that Richards wrote from her mother's grave. She dropped the letter and burst into tears. Slowly she regained her composure, took up the letter and read it; she wept as she read. She kept the messenger at her side for the rest of the evening, talking to him. She spoke of herself, of the shamefulness of her act and her mortification; she stated firmly, however, that she was not penitent. Nāhiʻenaʻena's tears had flowed quickly at the memory of her mother and for the hurt she had brought to her teacher, even for the shame brought upon herself. Tears came easily to her. Penitence, however, was something else; it was an imported, a foreign, attitude. How could she repent the union with her brother, the proper consummation to years of love?

In the presence of the courier, she wrote an answer to Richards. She addressed him with affection; she told him that what he had heard was true. Though she freely confessed her guilt and though she recognized she had destroyed her soul, she stipulated that her teacher must not come to her. This time, it appeared, she did not want to be "rescued."

Richards wrote two more letters to Nāhiʻenaʻena. They remained unanswered. He brooded about the marriage. He needed to explain it to himself. It was, after all, a mark of his failure. He came to the conclusion that the union was not impulsively or hastily entered into, that for some time Nāhiʻenaʻena had planned it. She had known only too well that her mission teachers and many of the chiefs would be horrified. But she had proceeded firmly—in command of her will for perhaps the last time—to carry out her dearest wish. Richards seems to have concluded that she accepted total responsibility.[16]

Nāhiʻenaʻena remained in Honolulu for several months. Only scant details survive concerning her activities. She and her brother went aboard a ship, where they were feted. When Hoapili and his wife returned to Lahaina in September, they urged her to accompany them; but the princess-queen refused. In the same month a missionary wrote one of his colleagues that she was under the care of a physician for a disease contracted because of her dissolute actions. By November the rumor had spread throughout the kingdom that she was pregnant by her brother. No record remains, however, of a child born within the appropriate period.[17]

Excommunication

A chant for Nāhiʻenaʻena recorded by Abraham Fornander proclaims: "The chiefs joined together the earth will be eternal. . . . While the chiefs join the earth abides firm." That was the old Hawaiʻi. In the changing Hawaiʻi, when chiefs joined together the earth trembled and cracked apart. A new order was rapidly being established.[1]

The marriage of the princess with Kauikeaouli was not officially recognized; the chiefs surrounding the royal pair, even those who had witnessed the ceremony, yielded to Western and Christian custom. The king continued to drink heavily and move restlessly about the island. For a while she drank too, and followed feverishly in his path. Then in mid-January of 1835, in what seems like an abrupt gesture, she returned in the company of Hoapili to Lahaina.[2]

Nāhiʻenaʻena was now twenty years old. She had become a tall, portly young woman who weighed about 200 pounds, typ-

ical in size, temperament, and willfulness of a princess of old
Hawai'i. And she had exiled herself to Lahaina, which she regarded as a desert, a prison. No longer simply a "dirty" place
which irritated, it aroused in her a spirit of defiance. Why did
she go back? We know that Hoapili and his wife had urged it.
Richards certainly wanted it. Nāhi'ena'ena, however, for several months after the "marriage" had been able to resist their
pleading and pressure. Finally she yielded.

She seems to have moved impulsively. Perhaps a kind of
desperation urged her, and a remembrance of long peaceful
days in the quiet of Lahaina, where she had once been celebrated in song and dance. Perhaps she hoped to escape de-
spair by returning to the home established for her by Keōpūolani and Hoapili. Perhaps she wanted to be near the tomb of
her mother. She might also have felt profound dismay as she
watched the dissolute course of her brother—a dismay
mingled with nostalgia for the days before the turmoil and the
shame.

Whatever the reasons, she returned; but there she found no
peace. A demon was in her. She openly defied missionary
teaching: she smoked, and played cards, often she was drunk
on rum or wine; she encouraged hula dances in her household.
She again took delight in interrupting church services. At one
meeting she talked and laughed during a sermon delivered by
Andrews on the theme "God is love." When the missionary
was nearly finished, she stood up, adjusted her skirt, then
"straddled out." It must have been magnificent straddling—
this proud, six-foot chiefess—with her attendants in her wake.
The congregation was perhaps both shocked and awed at her
daring.[3]

The demon flourished as she contrived ways to perplex and
irritate the missionaries. Mounted on a fine horse, she rode oc-

casionally up the hill to Lahainaluna, the school which the church had established for the Hawaiians and of which it was very proud. There, with the spell which from childhood she had cast over people, she talked graciously to the students. On one occasion she chatted with some who were thatching their workshop. Flattered by royal attention, they stopped work. Their wives were nearby, and the princess rode over to speak with them. After this visit, which was calculated to draw people to her, several students were eager to join the household of their chiefess. The missionaries were alarmed, especially as one of her retinue on that day had openly held a brandy bottle. Andrews complained that the people seemed to have forgotten that "she was a drunken, hardened, incestuous apostate."[4]

We may imagine how much William Richards suffered as he watched Nāhi'ena'ena during the months of her fall. What had gone wrong? He could not blame his Christian teaching or the premises of the Puritan ethic. Somehow, however, his work with this royal "lamb" had been unsuccessful. Probably Richards could not understand that he had been unable to touch that part of Nāhi'ena'ena's nature which would allow her to feel the dictates of conscience. She probably never grasped the conception of guilt in a Christian sense. Her own culture had taught her shame, and this shame might comfortably be transferred to Western religious attitudes. The deep interiority which serves guilt, however, demands a new conception of the self. This kind of selfhood Nāhi'ena'ena did not achieve. When Richards accepted the young chiefess into the church, he had been reasonably certain that her frequent religious questionings and her displays of devotion were testimony of true Christian feeling. He shared at times the intense desire of Stewart to create, as her mother had wished, a woman with the

148

spiritual qualities and gentleness of a missionary wife: and with the same humility. Not even Keōpūolani, however, had bowed to humility. The little girl had given Richards a hint of her resistance when she had told him that her heart was lifted up by the thought of the beautiful feather skirt which people were making for her; and that she at the same time was afraid. The conflict between feeling humility and being a princess was symbolized in the skirt. Charles Stewart, on his second visit to Hawai'i, saw clearly the perils for Nāhi'ena'ena. He recognized that the continual celebration of the princess must inevitably have its effect. For a chiefess from a long and sacred tradition, one still frequently honored in the old fashion, humility was probably impossible. Without humility, guilt was at best fluctuating.

At the time Nāhi'ena'ena returned to Maui, Richards was at the Wailuku station for a six-weeks' stay. In his concern over the reports which came to him, and his concern for the "lamb of his charge," he journeyed twice to Lahaina to see the princess. During the first visit, which lasted only a day, he sent her a letter saying that if she would give up her "wicked ways," he would once again become her teacher. She replied, but her answer was not satisfactory to him. She called in person; but he refused to see her because she had declined to accept all of his terms. He then returned to Wailuku; behind him he left a letter to be read in church which warned the people that they should shun "offending persons." On the second visit to Lahaina, he tried more direct pressure; he composed a letter of excommunication to be read the following Sunday. This threat made her weep. On the Sunday the letter was to be read, she sent a messenger to Richards stating that she would accede to all his demands. She begged for a stay of excommunication.

Soon after, Nāhiʻenaʻena talked with her teacher. He recorded that her conscience and judgment were on the side of religion, and she was frightened of excommunication. He was, however, filled with doubt. Her heart remained "unclean." After this meeting, she attempted for a while to conform to missionary ways — she abandoned cards, the hula, rum. The letter which had been read in church on the occasion of Richards' first visit to Lahaina reminded the people that the Scriptures commanded men to shun those who had offended it. The letter had its effect. Nāhiʻenaʻena was avoided by many Lahaina residents. And Richards wrote that "the countenance of hundreds as they pass her show that they consider the crown to have fallen from her head."[5]

She was now neither princess nor Christian woman to many of her own people. What was she to herself? There are no clues except in fragmentary accounts of her actions. While she was on Maui, she yielded to the coercion of the missionaries. They had held the final threat — excommunication. Her membership in the church mattered; Richards and Stewart mattered. But when in March she journeyed to the island of Hawaiʻi, the usual changes occurred.

The chiefs had continued their plans for Nāhiʻenaʻena to marry Leleiōhoku, and it was necessary for her to discuss with her fiancé and his guardian the final wedding arrangements. The missionaries stationed on Hawaiʻi kept what watch they could. They did not like what they heard and the little that they saw. Rumors came to them that she drank and played cards. At first she drank secretly; one letter records that she quietly sent a man to bring her fermented sugarcane and potato beer. Later she drank openly. She listened again to chants; they were of a special kind composed for and by the chiefs in which meanings were hidden so that not all listeners knew what they were hearing. The church records of Lahaina sum up her actions during February and March of 1835: she had shown signs of sincerity in her Christian behavior until her trip to Hawai'i. But on that island she was "guilty of intoxication and spent her nights in debauchery."[6]

The small colored artifacts of Nāhi'ena'ena's life, are like fragments of an old mosaic. We carefully fit together the bits we have, and a picture emerges with images in red and gold, with wreaths of flowers and feather coronets; with spelling slates and writing quills and churches; with images which tell myths of love, of death. Large areas of the mosaic, however, cannot be filled, empty spaces for which we no longer have the shining pieces. The details of her life are scant, often obscure, the patterns interrupted.

We know that after a two-month visit to Hawai'i she returned to Lahaina; the news of her fall from grace preceded her. There was no further doubt about excommunication for Nāhi'ena'ena; the mission prepared the formal letter. On May 23 the church members, many of them her own people, gathered to cast the crucial vote. When she heard, she rushed to Richards to request a further delay. Excommunication was still a frightening threat—her membership in the church had begun in childhood and had taken on meanings that might in some way have been related to early remembrances and the *mana* of the old culture. In the presence of Richards, however, she was still a willful chiefess. Her teacher, reinforced by the devout Hoapili, demanded that if she wanted a delay she must dismiss "her wicked companions." This she refused to do.

The letter of excommunication was read in the church on May 25. While the vote was being taken, Nāhi'ena'ena was drinking aboard a ship in Lahaina Roads. David Malo, scholar of Hawaiian antiquities, carried the document to her. He left no record of his call on the princess.[7]

If the church punished the princess by casting her out, it was nevertheless quite willing to accord her a church wedding. Her marriage to Leleiōhoku took place soon after her excommunication. Richards could not altogether abandon his royal "daughter." On the day of the wedding, Waineʻe Church, built by Hoapili in Lahaina, was filled. The commoners crowded to peer through the windows; others followed the royal couple to the church entrance. Nāhiʻenaʻena stepped for a moment into her accustomed role. She was a chiefess dressed in wedding finery; she was the center of ceremonial. Her heart must have been warmed by the large numbers of people who gathered to gaze at her and by the fact that William Richards performed the ceremony. The church-influenced newspaper *Ke Kumu Hawaii* sums up the feeling toward the young chiefs. "The people were concerned about their marriage and perhaps many of them that day had asked God to bless them." We do not know whether Kauikeaouli was present.[8]

Nothing is known of Nāhiʻenaʻena's life during the three months following her wedding. On the first day of September a ship was sent to bring her to Honolulu; Kauikeaouli was ill. She reached the capital on September 5. Leleiōhoku and the wife of Hoapili attended her. We have no record of this visit to Honolulu. By the first of the year 1836, the princess was back on Maui. She had returned to Wailuku, not Lahaina.[9]

15

"The Golden Bowl
Was Broken"

Princess Nāhiʻenaʻena had been born on the Kona coast of the "streaked and whispering sea," as an old song puts it. She had lived in Honolulu ("sheltered bay"), where she played her role as princess royal; she had dwelt in Lahaina ("cruel sun"), where her mission "fathers" had taught and prayed with her. Now she took her household to Wailuku ("waters of destruction"). Her behavior there suggests that rapidly the waters of destruction were moving to overwhelm her.

The resident missionary at Wailuku complained that Nāhiʻenaʻena was demoralizing his parishioners. The "wretched, polluted" young woman was "doing great mischief," he said. He was succeeded in 1835 by a missionary who viewed Nāhiʻenaʻena differently. The Reverend Richard Armstrong had come to Hawaiʻi with the fifth company of missionaries in 1832. Before going to Maui he had worked on the island of Molokaʻi. He had also spent a turbulent year in the Marquesas Islands. These experiences in the field and his own empathic nature apparently enabled him to reach some understanding of the Polynesian heart. A portrait painted at the time of his departure from New Bedford, Massachusetts, shows a man with large intent eyes, high cheekbones, and a slender mouth with full lower lip. The face is studious, yet it suggests a discriminating alertness.[1]

Armstrong observed Nāhiʻenaʻena for several months in Wailuku. He too reported that she had entered the waters of destruction. But his record shows compassion and insight. In a long, retrospective letter, Armstrong writes that when the princess first settled in Wailuku, she acted as if a "madness" possessed her heart. He perceived her rage, her defiance, her melancholy. She did not often attend church. When she did, however, she laughed and whispered, and invariably called attention to herself. At home she played cards and drank a good deal. Then, abruptly it seems, she became pious. Armstrong recognized this as merely an "external change in her conduct." Nāhiʻenaʻena put away her cards. She began to attend all church services regularly. She was thoughtful and quiet. Every Wednesday afternoon she went to Armstrong's school; in her home she established a school for the members of her household. She proclaimed a return to the *pono*, the right way. Her behavior, her words, as on so many earlier occasions, suggested a repentant heart. Yet Armstrong noticed that she was often "miserable and cast down." This was predictable—to become again a princess of piety was sufficient to induce melancholy and depression. As she had earlier written to Mrs. Stewart of her fluctuations, "thus it is continually."

Nāhiʻenaʻena frequently asked to see Armstrong. Each time he refused. "Considering how much she loves to be noticed and caressed," he wrote, "I thought it best to stand aloof from her until I was better satisfied of her sincerity." His methods were similar to those of Richards; both men attempted to use psychological coercion to bring their royal parishioner back into the fold. In addition to his refusal to see her, he devised another punishment. He told the church members in her retinue to remain faithful servants, but he instructed them to stay apart from the chiefess, not even to eat or drink or talk with her. The servants were to inform the princess of his advice. She took this cruel information "kindly"; she also wept.

As she could not meet him, Nāhiʻenaʻena tried to make overtures to Armstrong in her own way. "She has sent to me almost daily for one thing or another (a sure evidence in a Hawaiian of a desire to be friendly) such as books, quills, paper, etc. and has sent me frequently presents of fish in return. Thus you see how it is with this poor unhappy chief, once the idol of this nation."[2]

Armstrong clearly understood something of the deep conflict in Nāhiʻenaʻena, and in his restrained fashion, he showed sympathy. He could be sympathetic only in so far as his stern religious training would allow him. One wonders if he knew at that time a further perplexity for the princess — she was pregnant. It was, according to extant records, her first pregnancy.

In late April 1836, the king sailed on the brig *Becket* for Maui. He planned to bring his sister back to Honolulu for the birth of her child. Some speculated that the child must be Kauikeaouli's; others recognized that it could be Leleiōhoku's, for she was at that time about four months pregnant. Whoever might be the father, the king's journey had dynastic overtones. The birth would be an important event in the kingdom. The baby of Nāhiʻenaʻena would be next in line for the throne.[3]

The king and brother stayed on Maui for three or four

months. The missionaries reported that Kauikeaouli and Nāhi'ena'ena were frequently drunk. Stephen Reynolds records that although for everyone else the tabus were in effect—he probably meant the laws against drunkenness and adultery—"around the king and his sister . . . all is high life." Not only the missionaries watched from the sidelines. Two high chiefs also watched anxiously the behavior of their royal charges: Hoapili, who had made great efforts to preserve the sovereignty and dignity of the Kamehameha dynasty, and Kuakini, guardian of the princess' young husband. But even such venerable men as these could not, at times, interfere with the drunken royal will. They did not, however, withdraw from attendance on the king and his sister. Kauikeaouli and Nāhi'ena'ena had resumed the life they had shared briefly after their "marriage."[4]

In late August when the royal birth was imminent, Kauikeaouli took Nāhi'ena'ena to Honolulu. Hoapili and Leleiōhoku sailed with them. Nāhi'ena'ena was installed in a house built especially for her by Kīna'u, the *kuhina-nui*. It was constructed in the old way—a fenced compound in which stood many small grass houses and a very large one for the princess. Swarms of attendants and servants lived in these dwellings, idling their days away at cards, smoking, gossiping, and eating poi. Whenever Nāhi'ena'ena commanded, however, they were ready to serve. In her bedchamber, many persons were constantly gathered, ladies-in-waiting to fan her, attendants to hold the *kāhili* and royal spittoon. And, as had been true most of her life, fresh leis of flowers and leaves were brought each morning. The princess awaited her child in the public seclusion of the Hawaiian way.

We have no details about the birth of the baby. A stark statement, printed in the September 17 issue of *The Sandwich*

Island Gazette announced that the infant son of the Princess Nāhi'ena'ena died after a life of only a few hours. Had the child survived, it was noted, he would have been heir to the throne. The missionaries remained silent. But there was a Westerner who wrote of the princess at this time. This was W. S. W. Ruschenberger, a surgeon who was called in consultation by Dr. Rooke, the attending physician. Nāhi'ena'ena had remained seriously ill after the birth. The surgeon speculated that the illness was caused by the princess' "imprudently indulging in a cold bath" after the birth of the baby. If Nāhi'ena'ena had felt hot, she may have done just that; it was Hawaiian practice to cool the heat of fever in cold water.

Ruschenberger records two visits with Dr. Rooke to Nāhi'ena'ena. On the first, the two physicians arrived on horseback at the royal compound. A sentry held them at the gate until they could be properly announced. Outside the house of the princess stood a thatched shed where twenty or thirty people lounged on piles of fresh grass. One of the men came forward to take the horses, and the doctors entered the house. Ruschenberger writes that the floors and thatched roof were covered with mats. In an anteroom two chiefesses sat near a small table covered with a red cloth. They fanned themselves languidly and smoked short pipes. On the table were small gourds containing a few blades of grass: these were spittoons.

The king, dressed in a blue military jacket and white trousers, entered the anteroom to conduct the physicians to Nāhi'ena'ena. He led the way past a chintz screen into the bedchamber. The princess was lying on a soft mattress placed on a pile of fine mats. Over her "royal person" was a covering of white *kapa*. Her ladies-in-waiting and Leleiōhoku gently fanned her. Sprawled on the floor were several fat chiefs in shirts and trousers, who comforted themselves with either

157

pipes or poi. The king and Leleiōhoku revealed a deep anxiety for Nāhiʻenaʻena. This much Ruschenberger recorded.

On his second visit the doctor found that Nāhiʻenaʻena's bedroom had been redecorated. A sylvan atmosphere had been created as if she were vacationing in one of the cool valleys. Her servants had hung green boughs from the rafters. A pink satin counterpane bordered in black velvet was suspended above the bed. It hung in loose folds like a silken tent. The room was fragrant with the boughs and quantities of fresh flowers. The doctor writes that it ''might be compared to a grateful shade beneath some wide branching tree.'' The natural world to which she and all her people were close had been brought to her on her bed of sickness. The visitor and the princess had a short period of conversation. As Ruschenberger took his leave, Nāhiʻenaʻena said that his visit had helped her greatly, their talk had diverted her from pain. Before his departure, the attendants served him wine.[5]

Her illness continued through October and November. Chamberlain visited her and commented that she seemed to be quite low. He urged her to repentance. ''She did not appear to be perfectly stupid, but certainly not to be much awakened with the sense of her condition.'' These remarks and those of other missionaries indicate that in her illness the princess seemed torpid; she probably could not comprehend the seriousness of her physical condition, and certainly she had little feeling for the peril of her soul. In early November the chiefs were sufficiently worried to send for Dr. Judd, who was at that time in Lahaina.[6]

Nāhiʻenaʻena's condition grew worse in December, and the chiefs and missionaries gathered in traditional fashion. On December 30, 1836—Stephen Reynolds records that it was a ''beautiful morning''—Kauikeaouli, Leleiōhoku, Kīnaʻu, and the other high chiefs were close at her side. Mrs. Judd, who claims to have been there shortly before her death, wrote that the princess showed a deep distress about her past actions. "There is no mercy for an apostate," the dying young woman whispered; "I am one." Mrs. Judd reminded her that Jesus on the Cross had promised pardon to those who were penitent. "Do you say so?" the princess asked. "Can there be hope for one who has sinned as I have?" She made an effort to plead for mercy. But she could speak no longer. In Mrs. Judd's words, "the golden bowl was broken." It is difficult to say today whether the zealous Mrs. Judd really heard those words from the dying princess, or whether she indulged a kind of wishful fantasy of final repentance.[7]

A great stillness filled Honolulu. A single gun announced the death of the princess. By evening, the wailing had begun. Kauikeaouli in his grief recited the birth chant of Nāhiʻena-ʻena; and he cried out that he alone—he who had counted on the companionship of his sister—was left to rule the kingdom. He ordered that his sister's body be removed to the palace to lie in state. Her coffin was placed on a feather cloak. Over it was hung a pall of crimson velvet. A brass plate on the lid recorded her name, her age, and the date of her death. Above the plate a crown had been fashioned of brass nails. Prominently displayed was her feather skirt, a symbol of her rank; and a symbol, ironically, which held connotations of the dilemma and anguish of her life.[8]

Two ceremonies were held for Nāhiʻenaʻena. The first, in Honolulu, was a traditional procession of the great chiefs and other distinguished people. The simple cart draped in black silk carrying her coffin was escorted by the brilliantly colored state *kāhili* and funereal ones of black feathers. At the church,

Hiram Bingham conducted the services. In his sermon he recalled the many good deeds and words of Nāhiʻenaʻena; and he said he had no doubt she had died a penitent believer in the Christian faith. After the ceremony, a salute was fired from the fort and ships in the harbor.[9]

The second funeral was held in early April on Maui. Kauikeaouli made elaborate preparations. He fitted out a ship to carry his sister to the tomb of their mother and ordered a royal road to be cut through the groves of *kou* and breadfruit at Lahaina—a winding promenade leading first toward the mountains and then back toward the sea. Its surface was many-layered: first sand, then grass, and finally mats—like a royal highway of ancient times. The cortege moved along it; the great chiefs, men bearing the *kāhili* of state shimmering yellow, green, and red in the sun, and finally the coffin somberly draped in black. As close as they dared, the commoners gathered and wailed. When the service of prayer began, all lamentation ceased.[10]

The shock of Nāhiʻenaʻena's death put an abrupt end, for a time at least, to Kauikeaouli's restlessness and dissipation. He turned his mind to the obligations and responsibilities of kingship. Mrs. Judd wrote that ''since the death of his sister the king appears sober and thoughtful.'' Kamakau reported that the young ruler meditated about the teachings of the Christians. He remembered the laws he had established for the welfare of his people, laws that he himself had broken. He felt he could not bury Nāhiʻenaʻena until he had improved himself. Thus, according to Kamakau, he took a consort as a first step into the new and more serious phase of his role as king. Though he had never joined the Christian church, he married his favorite chiefess, Kalama, in a Christian ceremony per-

160

formed by Hiram Bingham. Stephen Reynolds gives us a glimpse of the mood at the wedding: "No noise, no talk, very still."

After the Maui funeral, the king continued to live in Lahaina for about eight years. James Jarves, an early traveler in Polynesia, comments that he selected this village so that he could be farther away from the influence of foreigners and live more intimately among his chiefs. Kamakau writes that he remained in Lahaina out of love for his sister. The two reasons seem to have mingled in the mind of the king—probably with others which remain hidden from us. Kauikeaouli had suddenly to confront the fact that he could not share his life or his kingdom with his sister; this painful reality cut deep, stirring the thoughtful, melancholy side of his nature. His sister was the woman he had most loved.[11]

In Lahaina he built a large stone house, and on the top floor he created a mausoleum for his mother, his sister, and her child. Unlike the usual mausoleum, this one was filled with light; its windows looked out at the mountains, its doors opened onto a verandah facing the sea. He furnished the room in handsome fashion. Mirrors gleamed on the walls. A small organ was installed, on which he played occasionally for visitors. In the center of the room stood a huge bedstead on which lay the coffins covered in scarlet silk velvet. Around the bed great *kāhili* turned their feathers in the sea wind. Against one wall was a glass cabinet in which was arranged a display of Nāhiʻenaʻena's clothes—dresses, satin slippers, a black lace veil ornamented with pink and green silk flowers, a white silk cape. This was not a Western morbidity. The clothes of chiefs were sacred, they contained *mana*. And for the king they contained remembrance. He frequently took visitors into the room to see the "tomb" of his family.[12]

161

The king each year set aside several days for celebration of the life and death of the Princess Nāhiʻenaʻena — she who had been his sister and, for a time, his unrecognized queen; she who in death had become a symbol of the destiny of the Hawaiian people, though Kauikeaouli could not know the extent of the symbolism of her life. He clung to his memories; he kept her image fresh in the minds of his people.

Nāhiʻenaʻena was born into the world of the past. "Beautiful are the chiefs as the ebb and flow of tides." So runs a chant for the princess. She lived in a changing world when Hawaiʻi first observed and then accepted Western manners and attitudes. Where was there a firm footing for her? How could she tread majestically as had chiefesses for centuries past? Her life foreshadowed the increasing dilemma of the Hawaiian people. They wanted to preserve roots in the ancient subtleties of Polynesian culture; they also yearned for the skills and the new excitement brought by foreigners. The intermingling of bloods was easier than the intermingling of cultures. Nāhiʻenaʻena, by Western fiat, had not been allowed to preserve the purity of her sacred blood; today Hawaiians watch their racial stream dissolve into the blend of the many people who have come to their islands. The princess, in a sense, was a plaything of history, a child of destiny. She was heiress of a long, brilliant past in the Pacific; she was the uncertain harbinger of the future. The double canoe sails on, with hesitation.

ᘒ Notes ᘓ

Abbreviations

AH Archives of Hawaii
HMCS Hawaiian Mission Children's Society
MH *Missionary Herald*
ML Missionary Letters (see Bibliography)
UH Hawaiian Collection, Sinclair Library, University of Hawaii

CHAPTER 1. "My Precious Object"

1. Nathaniel B. Emerson, *Unwritten Literature of Hawaii*, p. 209.
2. Abraham Fornander, "Fornander Collection of Hawaiian Antiquities and Folk-lore," vol. 6, pp. 438–443.
3. Ibid., pp. 444–450.

CHAPTER 2. The "Well-Behaved Child"

1. For the greater part of this chapter I am indebted to Charles Stewart, *A Residence in the Sandwich Islands*, pp. 68–94; and Hiram Bingham, *A Residence of Twenty-one Years in the Sandwich Islands*, pp. 183–186.

163

2. *Missionary Album*, pp. 184–187; Bradford Smith, *Yankees in Paradise*, pp. 98–99.

CHAPTER 3.   Keōpūolani, Sacred Mother

1. S. M. Kamakau, *Ruling Chiefs of Hawaii*, p. 260; S. D. Alexander, *A Brief History of the Hawaiian People*, p. 218.
2. Kamakau, *Ruling Chiefs*, p. 260; Alexander, *History*, p. 158.
3. Kamakau, *Ruling Chiefs*, p. 260.
4. Ibid., pp. 263–264.
5. [William Richards], *Memoir of Keopuolani*, p. 2. Kamakau says she was born in 1780.
6. Kamakau, *Ruling Chiefs*, p. 263; S. M. Kamakau, *Ka Po'e Kahiko*, p. 5; Kamakau, *Ruling Chiefs*, p. 259.
7. Kamakau, *Ka Po'e Kahiko*, p. 85.
8. Kamakau, *Ruling Chiefs*, pp. 259, 260, 208.
9. Ibid., p. 261; Richards, *Keopuolani*, p. 14.
10. Kamakau, *Ruling Chiefs*, p. 224.
11. Sheldon Dibble, *History of the Sandwich Islands*, pp. 149–151.
12. Kamakau, *Ruling Chiefs*, p. 261.

CHAPTER 4.   "Dark Heart"

1. Kamakau, *Ruling Chiefs*, p. 250.
2. Maria Loomis, Journal.
3. Bingham, *Residence*, p. 183.
4. Ibid.
5. Richards, *Memoir*, p. 18.
6. Ibid., pp. 18–19.
7. Bingham, *Residence*, p. 192.
8. Stewart, *Residence*, pp. 131, 134–135.
9. Ibid., p. 136.
10. Ibid., p. 142.
11. Ibid., pp. 143–144.
12. Ibid., pp. 144–145.
13. William Ellis, *Polynesian Researches, Hawaii*, pp. 78–79.
14. This account of Liholiho's visit to Lahaina is recorded in Stewart, *Residence*, pp. 147–150.

CHAPTER 5.   First Fruit of the Mission

1. Stewart, *Residence*, pp. 159–160.

2. Ibid., p. 160.
3. Ibid., p. 162.
4. Stewart, *Residence*, p. 170; Richards, *Memoir*, p. 30.
5. Stewart, *Residence*, p. 170; Richards, *Memoir*, pp. 31–33.
6. Richards, *Memoir*, pp. 32, 34–35; Stewart, *Residence*, p. 165.
7. Stewart, *Residence*, pp. 166–167.
8. Ibid., pp. 170–171.
9. Ibid., pp. 171–172.
10. Richards, *Memoir*, p. 37.
11. Stewart, *Residence*, pp. 172–174.

CHAPTER 6.   In the Absence of the King

1. Kamakau, *Ruling Chiefs*, p. 255; Frank Pleadwell, "Voyage to England of King Liholiho and Queen Kamamalu," pp. 1–2.
2. Ellis, *Polynesian Researches*, pp. 446–447.
3. Kamakau, *Ruling Chiefs*, pp. 255–256; Pleadwell, p. 2; Bingham, pp. 202–203.
4. Kamakau, *Ruling Chiefs*, pp. 256–257; Bingham, pp. 203–204.
5. Stewart, *Residence*, pp. 197–198, 199–200.
6. MH, vol. 20, p. 280.
7. ML, vol. 2, p. 712a.
8. Elisha Loomis, Journal, pp. 15–16.
9. Kamakau, *Ruling Chiefs*, p. 315.
10. Stewart, *Residence*, pp. 240–247.
11. MH, vol. 22, p. 39; Lord Byron, *Voyage of H.M.S. Blonde to the Sandwich Islands in the Years 1824–1825*, pp. 246–247.
12. Byron, *Voyage of H.M.S. Blonde*, p. 247.
13. ML, vol. 2, p. 725a; MH, vol. 22, pp. 143–144.
14. The translation of Toteta's journal was published in MH, vol. 22, pp. 170–172.
15. MH, vol. 22, p. 145.
16. Ibid., p. 149.

CHAPTER 7.   *Aliʻi* in London

1. For most of chapter 7, I am indebted to Pleadwell, "Voyage to England"; to Alfred Frankenstein, *The Royal Visitors*; and to Byron, *Voyage of H.M.S. Blonde*.
2. British Public Records Office, F.O. 58/3, from Ralph S. Kuykendall, *The Hawaiian Kingdom 1788–1854*, p. 79.

CHAPTER 8.   The Boy-King

1. Levi Chamberlain, Journal, vol. 4, pp. 38–39.
2. Stewart, *Residence*, pp. 272–273.
3. William Richards, in Stewart, *Residence*, pp. 277–278.
4. Robert Dampier, *To the Sandwich Islands on H.M.S. Blonde*, ed. Pauline King Joerger, p. 34.
5. Stewart, *Residence*, pp. 278–279.
6. Ibid., pp. 279–282; Bingham, *Residence*, pp. 264–265.
7. Dampier, *To the Sandwich Islands*, pp. 36, 43.
8. Kuykendall, *Hawaiian Kingdom*, p. 119; Kamakau, *Ruling Chiefs*, p. 258.

CHAPTER 9.   Child of God

1. Kamakau, *Ruling Chiefs*, p. 320.
2. Chamberlain, Journal, vol. 5, pp. 50–54, 59.
3. Ibid., vol. 7, pp. 2, 8; Bingham, *Residence*, pp. 313–314.
4. ML, vol. 2, p. 756a; Records of the Church at Lahaina.
5. Kuykendall, *Hawaiian Kingdom*, pp. 122–123; Chamberlain, Journal, vol. 8, pp. 14–21, 27, 29; Bingham, *Residence*, pp. 314–318.
6. Chamberlain, Journal, vol. 8, p. 30; Stephen Reynolds, Journal, Dec. 15, 1827; Jan. 10, 1828.

CHAPTER 10.   "Where the Lava Gathered"

1. Kamakau, *Ruling Chiefs*, pp. 283–284.
2. Emerson, *Unwritten Literature*, p. 187.
3. Kamakau, *Ruling Chiefs*, p. 284.
4. Stewart, pp. 302, 305–307.
5. Kamakau, *Ruling Chiefs*, p. 284.
6. Emerson, *Unwritten Literature*, pp. 231, 187.
7. John Papa Ii, *Fragments of Hawaiian History*, p. 169.
8. Laura Fish Judd, *Honolulu*, p. 20.
9. Chamberlain, Journal, vol. 9, p. 28.
10. This account of the journey around Maui is taken from ML, vol. 3, pp. 873–878; Chamberlain, Journal, vol. 10, pp. 6–8, 11, 13.
11. Chamberlain, Journal, vol. 10, p. 5.
12. Ibid., vol. 11, pp. 19–25.

CHAPTER 11.   "Thus It Is Continually"

1. Chamberlain, Journal, vol. 12, pp. 7, 24–25.

2. Bingham, *Residence*, pp. 343–346; Chamberlain, Journal, vol. 12, pp. 27–29.

3. Chamberlain, Journal, vol. 13, p. 8.

4. C. S. Stewart, *A Visit to the South Seas*, vol. 2, p. 62.

5. Ibid., pp. 113, 115, 120–121.

6. Ibid., pp. 121–132.

7. Ibid., pp. 156–157.

8. Ibid., p. 192.

9. Ibid., pp. 192–194.

10. Ibid., p. 194.

11. Ibid., p. 160.

12. Ibid., p. 195.

13. Ibid., p. 160.

14. Ibid., pp. 200–201, 194.

15. Ibid., pp. 195–196.

16. Ibid., pp. 196–198.

17. Navy Department Archives, Captain French's Cruise in the U.S.S. *Vincennes*, 1826–1830.

18. Stewart, *South Seas*, pp. 169, 172–173, 222.

19. Ibid., pp. 222–226.

20. Ibid., pp. 227–229.

21. Ibid., pp. 177–178.

22. Ibid., pp. 178–179.

23. Ibid., pp. 180–181.

24. Ibid., pp. 181–183.

25. Ibid., pp. 234–235.

CHAPTER 12.   "The Brink of Destruction"

1. Andrews to Chamberlain, Aug. 20, 1829, HMCS.

2. Richards to Chamberlain, Oct. 27, 1830, HMCS.

3. Records of the Church at Lahaina; Richards to Chamberlain, Feb. 20, 1832, HMCS; Chamberlain, Journal, vol. 15, pp. 51, 54.

4. Bingham, *Residence*, pp. 431–434.

5. Kamakau, *Ruling Chiefs*, pp. 308–309.

6. Bingham, *Residence*, p. 436.

7. Chamberlain, Journal, vol. 17, pp. 19–30.

8. Ibid., p. 31; Kuykendall, *Hawaiian Kingdom*, p. 134; Bingham, *Residence*, pp. 447–448.

9. Richards to Ruggles, Jan. 2, 1833, HMCS.

10. Chamberlain, Journal, vol. 17, p. 23.

11. Richards to Chamberlain, April 2, 1833, HMCS.
12. Chamberlain, Journal, vol. 17, p. 41.
13. Ibid., pp. 43–47; Kamakau, *Ruling Chiefs*, p. 336.

CHAPTER 13. Brother and Sister

1. Abraham Russell to the King, Lahaina, Aug. 2, 1831, AH; George W. C. Jones, "The History of Kamehameha King," *Pacific Commercial Advertiser*, March 27, 1875.
2. *Pacific Commercial Advertiser*, March 27, 1875; Kamehameha V, Chamberlain's Accounts, 1867–1868, AH.
3. Sereno E. Bishop to Gilman, Honolulu, June 5, 1901, Sereno E. Bishop Letter Book, number 2.
4. Andrews to Chamberlain, Jan. 6, 1834, HMCS.
5. ML, vol. 6, pp. 1634–1635.
6. Richards to Chamberlain, Jan. 8, 1834, HMCS.
7. Chamberlain, Journal, vol. 18, p. 11.
8. Ibid., pp. 15–16.
9. G. P. Judd in L. Judd, *Honolulu*, p. 191.
10. Chamberlain, Journal, vol. 18, pp. 12, 17.
11. Kamakau, *Ruling Chiefs*, p. 339.
12. Stephen Reynolds, Journal, June 8, 1834; June 9, 1834.
13. Chamberlain, Journal, vol. 18, p. 23.
14. Ibid., p. 26; Hitchcock Papers; Gavan Daws, *Shoal of Time*, p. 94; Reynolds, Journal, July 22, 1834. Quotations from the Reynolds Journal are used with the permission of the Peabody Museum of Salem, Mass.
15. Chamberlain, Journal, vol. 18, p. 26; ML, vol. 6, pp. 1636–1637.
16. ML, vol. 6, pp. 1636–1637; Records of the Church at Lahaina, July 22, 1834.
17. Chapin to Ruggles, Sept. 30, 1834, HMCS; S. Reynolds, Journal, Aug. 6, 1834.

CHAPTER 14. Excommunication

1. Fornander, *Hawaiian Antiquities*, p. 444.
2. Chamberlain, Journal, vol. 19, p. 9.
3. Andrews to Chamberlain, Jan. 19, 1835, HMCS.
4. Ibid.
5. ML, vol. 4, pp. 1655–1656; Chapin to Chamberlain, Jan. 8, 1835, HMCS.
6. Baldwin to Chamberlain, March 22, 1835, HMCS.

7. Records of the Church at Lahaina; ML, vol. 6, p. 1658; Chamberlain, Journal, vol. 19, p. 19.

8. Kamakau, *Ruling Chiefs*, p. 340; *Ke Kumu Hawaii*, July 1835, p. 20.

9. Chamberlain, Journal, vol. 19, p. 27.

CHAPTER 15. "The Golden Bowl Was Broken"

1. ML, vol. 6, pp. 1756 1757; *Missionary Album*, pp. 30-31.

2. ML, vol. 8, 22301-22302.

3. Chamberlain, Journal, vol. 20, p. 14.

4. Reynolds, Journal, July 3, 1836; Coan to Chamberlain, July 14, 1836, HMCS; Baldwin to Chamberlain, Aug. 13, 1836, HMCS.

5. W. S. W. Ruschenberger, *Narrative of a Voyage Round the World*, vol. 2, pp. 330-334.

6. Chamberlain, Journal, vol. 20,   p. 26.

7. L. Judd, *Honolulu*, pp. 48-49.

8. Kamakau, *Ruling Chiefs*, p. 341; Reynolds, Journal, Jan. 12, 1837.

9. Bingham, *Residence*, pp. 498-499.

10. Kamakau, *Ruling Chiefs*, p. 342.

11. Ibid.

12. Mary Ives to Mrs. Amona Rossiter, Jan. 21, 1838, HMCS; Andelusia Condé, Journal, Dec. 11, 1837.

≈ Bibliography ≈

Only those sources cited in the notes are listed. In the case of manuscript material, the repository is named. For manuscript material outside the Hawaiian Islands, the repository is listed followed by the place in Hawai'i where a microfilm is available. Abbreviations are listed on the first page of the notes section.

Alexander, W. D. *A Brief History of the Hawaiian People*. New York: American Book Co., 1899.

Bingham, Hiram. *A Residence of Twenty-one Years in the Sandwich Islands*. New York: Sherman Converse, 1848.

Bishop, Sereno E. Letter Book. Manuscript. HMCS.

Byron, George Anson, Captain the Right Honorable Lord. *Voyage of H.M.S. Blonde to the Sandwich Islands in the Year 1824–1825*. London, 1826.

Chamberlain, Levi. Journal. Manuscript; typescript (in 22 vols.). HMCS. (Volume and page references in the notes are to the typescript version.)

Condé, Andelusia. Journal. Manuscript. HMCS.

Dampier, Robert. *To the Sandwich Islands on H.M.S. Blonde*. Edited by Pauline King Joerger. Honolulu: The University Press of Hawaii, 1971.

Daws, Gavan. *Shoal of Time.* New York: Macmillan, 1968. Reprint. Honolulu: The University Press of Hawaii, 1974.

Dibble, Sheldon. *History of the Sandwich Islands.* Lahainaluna, 1843.

Ellis, William. *Polynesian Researches, Hawaii.* Rutland, Vt.: Charles E. Tuttle, 1969.

Emerson, Nathaniel B. *Unwritten Literature of Hawaii: The Sacred Songs of the Hula.* Rutland, Vt.: Charles E. Tuttle, 1965. (First published as *Bulletin of the Bureau of American Ethnology* 38, Washington, D. C., 1909.)

Frankenstein, Alfred. *The Royal Visitors.* Portland: Oregon Historical Society, 1963.

Fornander, Abraham. "Fornander Collection of Hawaiian Antiquities and Folk-lore." *Memoirs of the Bernice P. Bishop Museum*, vol. 6 (1919).

Hitchcock Papers, Manuscript. Almeda Goss Deposit. HMCS.

Ii, John Papa. *Fragments of Hawaiian History.* Honolulu: Bishop Museum Press, 1963.

Jones, George W. C. "The History of Kamehameha King." Manuscript. Theresa Bowler Hughes Collection, AH.

Judd, Laura Fish. *Honolulu.* Honolulu: The Honolulu Star-Bulletin, 1963.

Kamakau, S. M. *Ka Poʻe Kahiko; The People of Old.* Translated by Mary Kawena Pukui; edited by Dorothy B. Barrère. Honolulu: Bishop Museum Press, 1964.

————*Ruling Chiefs of Hawaii.* Honolulu: The Kamehameha Schools Press, 1961.

Kuykendall, Ralph S. *The Hawaiian Kingdom, 1788-1854: Foundation and Transformation.* Honolulu: The University of Hawaii, 1938.

Loomis, Elisha. Journal. Manuscript, HMCS. Typescript, HMCS, UH.

Loomis, Maria. Journal. Manuscript; typescript. HMCS.

Missionary Album, Portraits and Biographical Sketches of the American Protestant Missionaries to the Hawaiian Islands. Honolulu: HMCS, 1969.

Missionary Herald. A periodical. Boston.

Missionary Letters from the Sandwich Island Mission to American Board of Commissioners for Foreign Missions, 1819-1837. 8 vols. Typescript. HMCS.

Pacific Commercial Advertiser. A newspaper. Honolulu.

Pleadwell, Frank. "Voyage to England of King Liholiho and Queen Kamamalu." Typescript. UH. 1952.

Records of the Church at Lahaina. Manuscript. HMCS.

Reynolds, Stephen. Journal. Manuscript, Peabody Museum, Salem, Mass.: microfilm, HMCS.

[Richards, William]. *Memoir of Keopuolani*. Boston: Crocker & Brewster, 1825.

Ruschenberger, W. S. W. *Narrative of a Voyage Round the World*. London, 1838.

Sandwich Island Gazette. A newspaper. Honolulu.

Smith, Bradford. *Yankees in Paradise*. New York: J. B. Lippincott, 1956.

Stewart, Charles. *A Residence in the Sandwich Islands*. Boston: Weeks, Jordan and Co., 1839.

———*A Visit to the South Seas*. New York: John P. Haven, 1831.

❦ Index ❧

This book was composed on the Unified Composing System at The University Press of Hawaii. Text design is by Roger J. Eggers and the typeface is Bodoni Book. Display matter is set in Tiffany Light.

Text paper is Perkins & Squier Vellum Offset, basis 55. Offset printed and bound by Halliday Lithograph Corporation.